The Italian Economy in the 1990s

This study examines Italy's structural changes in the 1990s, tracing the economic developments as well as the measures that were introduced in this period together with their implications. It portrays some of the fundamental reforms in the labour market and their economic consequences, analyses the debt position and tracks down developments on the privatization front. It also reveals the economic consequences of the devaluation of the lira following Italy's exit from the ERM.

The Italian Economy in the 1990s presents an authoritative and up-to-date account of one of Europe's major economies. Rich in data, it provides analyses of:

- Italy's economic performance
- the labour market
- public debt
- privatization

H. M. Scobie is Executive Director of the European Economics and Financial Centre, London and Professor of Economics, University of London. Author of numerous books and articles, she was editor of the *International Studies in Economic Modelling* series (Chapman and Hall), now relaunched as *New International Studies in Economic Modelling* (Routledge). **S. Mortali**, **S. Persaud** and **P. Docile** are staff economists of the European Economics and Financial Centre, London.

The Italian Economy in the 1990s

H. M. Scobie, S. Mortali,
S. Persaud and P. Docile

European Economics and Financial Centre, London

European Economics and Financial Centre

London and New York

First published 1996
by Routledge
11 New Fetter Lane, London EC4P 4EE

Simultaneously published in the USA and Canada
by Routledge
29 West 35th Street, New York, NY 10001

Typeset in Times by
Keystroke, Jacaranda Lodge, Wolverhampton

Printed and bound in Great Britain by
TJ Press (Padstow) Ltd, Padstow, Cornwall

British Library Cataloguing in Publication Data
A catalogue record for this book is available from the British Library

Library of Congress Cataloguing in Publication Data
A catalogue record for this book has been requested

ISBN 0–415–13936–8

Contents

Figures

Tables

Acknowledgements

We wish to thank the following for their valuable time for discussions in relation to the preparation of this study and for their valuable comments, though they remain in no way responsible for the contents of this document.

Professor Mario Draghi, Director General, Italian Treasury.

Professor Alberto Giovannini, Chairman of the Council of Economic Advisors, Italian Treasury (up to September 1994).

Professor Lorenzo Pecchi, Council of Economic Advisors, Italian Treasury.

Dr Ignazio Visco, Head of the Research Department, Bank of Italy.

Dr Gian Paolo Galli, Head of the International Research Department, Bank of Italy.

Dr Paola Casavolla, Research Department, Bank of Italy.

Dr Sandro Trento, Research Department, Bank of Italy.

Dr Giovanni Magnoni, Research Department, Bank of Italy.

Dr Ignazio Angeloni, Research Department, Bank of Italy.

Dr Carlo Andrea Bollino, ISPE.

Dr Stefano Micossi, Head of Centro Studi Confindustria.

Dr Paolo Annunziato, Centro Studi Confindustria.

Dr Ugo Inzerillo, Centro Studi Confindustria.

Mrs Nardoni, Centro Studi Confindustria.

All the errors and omissions in this study remain our responsibility.

1 Executive summary

This study examines Italy's structural changes in the 1990s, tracing the economic developments as well as the measures that were introduced in this period, together with their implications. It portrays some of the fundamental reforms in the labour market and their economic consequences, analyses the debt position and tracks down developments on the privatization front. It also reveals the economic consequences of the devaluation of the lira following its exit from the ERM.

While the world financial market has been preoccupied with the political sustainability of Italian leadership, the real side of the economy has had a strong performance which has been ignored by the market. Among these are the following:

- GDP growth between the first and second quarters of 1994 was the highest in the European Union at 5.6 per cent.
- Inflation came down to a 25-year low of 3.6 per cent (August 1994).
- There has been a 16 per cent rise in the industrial production index in August 1994.
- Investment has increased greatly – with a 13.9 per cent increase in Equipment Investment between Q4 1993 and Q1 1994.
- The government's 'primary' budget balance (i.e. excluding the expense of interest payment) went into surplus in 1992. It was also the only G7 country to achieve a surplus position in 1993. The primary surplus has remained in surplus in 1994.
- On the external side, the current account has swung from a deficit of 2 per cent of GDP in 1992 to a surplus of around 2 per cent in the first half of 1994.

The Italian labour market has traditionally had many problems which have been gradually addressed in the 1990s. Even though unemployment still stands at 11 per cent in the mid-1990s, the steps already taken are likely to have beneficial effects on the unemployment figures in the future. The main features of the labour market reforms introduced in the first half of the 1990s were as follows:

- the removal of barriers *vis-à-vis* hiring regulations. Since 1991 firms have been able to decide autonomously whom to hire
- the abolition of the wage indexation system, *scala mobile*, the last payment of which was made in November 1991, though officially it was only abolished in July 1992
- the revamping of the old and introduction of a substantially improved wage bargaining scheme in 1993
- the establishment of an insurance system for the purpose of mass redundancy.

Although much progress has been made removing some of the barriers in the working of the labour market in the 1990s, there are still improvements to be made in making it more efficient and reducing unemployment. The recession of 1992–3, which led to much industry rationalization and many business closures, in fact added to the unemployment problem, increasing it from 9.8 per cent in 1992 to a peak of 11 per cent in the summer of 1994. The full benefits of the labour market reforms will take a period of time to work their way through the economy.

The problem of Italian public debt remains. The greatest obstacle to the recovery of the Italian fiscal position is without doubt the massive interest payment, which at 12 per cent of GDP in 1993 accounted for the entire borrowing requirement. By the end of 1994 the state sector debt is estimated to have reached 123 per cent of GDP (as stated in the Treasury Budget for the years 1995–7, presented to Parliament in the autumn of 1994). Moreover, the state sector borrowing requirement is estimated by the Treasury to have dropped to 10.2 per cent of GDP in 1994. This is a significant improvement given the high borrowing levels of around 14 per cent recorded during the mid-1980s. Despite the recession of 1992–3 considerable effort has been made to enforce budgetary restraint in order to meet the criteria set out by the Maastricht Treaty.

The fiscal retrenchment has primarily taken the form of spending cuts in the areas of health and pensions and through a rationalization of the local government system. A positive primary balance achieved from 1992 onwards is a trend that is expected to continue during the second half of the 1990s. Moreover, a large part of Italian government debt matures in 1995 and 1996. In these conditions, Italy's state indebtedness is expected to peak in 1995 or 1996 at 124–125 per cent of GDP and fall to 121 per cent in 1997.

Italy's programme for the sale of state shareholdings in industry and service sectors initiated in January 1992 became effective in late 1993. At the same time, important reorganizational measures were carried out in many public-sector enterprises as well as the establishment of a Permanent Committee for Privatizations or the Regulatory Authority for public utilities. The Italian government entered the operational phase of privatization in June 1993, selling the 95 per cent controlling interests in *Siv* (an *Efim* subsidiary). Subsequently the following privatizations took place: *Credito Italiano* in December 1993, *Imi* in February 1994, *Banca Commerciale Italiana* in March 1994 and the state insurance company *Ina* in June 1994. By 1995 the total capital raised through privatizations was over 14.5 trillion lire.

The transformation of public enterprises into limited companies will continue into the second half of the 1990s. These actions will be accompanied by a number of measures regarding the regulation and liberalization of services. Among the scheduled privatizations of 1995 are: the *Iri*-owned telecommunication company Stet, the Treasury-owned electricity company *Enel*, the Foundation-owned bank *Cariplo* and the Treasury-owned energy and engineering company *Eni/Agip*; with these the government hopes to raise approximately 100,000 billion lire.

Overall, the Italian economy has made rapid progress in many areas in the 1990s. This positive trend should continue to make the future for Italy quite encouraging, for many of the measures taken in the first half of the 1990s will be working their way through the economy in the second half of the decade.

Study co-sponsored by the Swiss Bank Corporation.

2   Economic performance

2.1 INTRODUCTION

Italy has undergone a process of restructuring in the 1990s with a resulting economic performance that has compared favourably with the rest of its European partners. By 1994 it has been able to out-perform many of the EU member states on the real side of the economy. It has achieved both low inflation and deceleration of wages – the latter being attributable mainly to the abolition of *scala mobile*, the wage indexation system. Devaluing the lira in September 1992 aided an export boost after 1993 without any inflationary pressure on the economy. The huge public sector debt (at 123 per cent of GDP) remains a major problem It is this significant variable that prevents Italy from meeting the Maastricht criterion of 60 per cent ratio of debt to GDP. However, due to the short-term nature and composition of the debt, some of the public debt comes to maturity in 1995 and 1996. Hence, there should be a levelling-off in the size of the debt in the mid-1990s – constraining the steep growth it has experienced in the late 1980s and early 1990s.

Moreover, a series of privatizations of nationalized enterprises began in 1993. Since June 1993, seven previously state-owned enter-prises have been privatized, raising a total of more than L13,000 bn. The biggest privatizations are yet to take place, and should boost the fledgling stock market. *Stet*, the telecommunications company; *Enel*, the electricity generation company; and *Eni/Agip* are among the companies to be sold in the next round of privatizations.

2.2 OUTPUT OF THE ECONOMY

The rise in Italian GDP between the first and second quarters of 1994 (at 5.6 per cent) has been the fastest in the European Union, surpassing

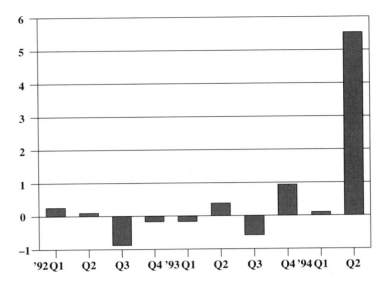

Figure 2.1 GDP growth 1992–4, % change on previous quarter
Source: Istat (Istituto Nazionale di Statistica)

even the government's own forecasts. This spectacular growth has been the result of an upturn in domestic demand which gradually gained momentum after the recession of 1992–3. The recovery of the Italian economy before this was predominantly export-led, helped by the increased competitiveness of the lira after the devaluation in September 1992, when the lira made an exit from the ERM.

Table 2.1 GDP at market prices, 1988–93

	1989	1990	1991	1992	1993
Total (L.bn) at current prices	1,193,463	1,312,067	1,429,453	1,504,323	1,560,114
at constant 1985 prices	921,714	941,387	952,685	959,814	953,445
real % change	2.9	2.1	1.2	0.7	– 0.7

Source: OECD, Quarterly National Accounts 1993.

During 1992–3, owing to the recession that hit the economy, output fell and the level of GDP dropped by –0.7 per cent. This was the first actual annual fall in the output level since 1975. The recession actually began in the last quarter of 1992 and showed signs of ending in the last quarter of 1993. In 1994 this upturn gathered pace as domestic demand started to improve and exports continued to rise. In 1993, the net export increase had not been sufficient to overcome the effects of falling domestic demand. However, in 1994 with domestic demand stimulated, the combined effect of export growth and improved domestic demand began to improve the output figures with GDP showing a remarkable 5.6 per cent growth in Q2 over Q1. The year-on-year GDP growth was 1.5 per cent in Q1 and 2.3 per cent in Q2 during 1994. The average GDP growth over the three months (August–October 1994) compared to the previous three months (May–July) is 5.7 per cent, which also suggests that growth is continuing.

Table 2.2 GDP growth, 1992–4

1992				1993				1994	
Q1	Q2	Q3	Q4	Q1	Q2	Q3	Q4	Q1	Q2
0.2	0.1	–0.8	–0.2	–0.2	0.3	–0.6	0.9	0.1	2.3

Source: Istat (Istituto Nazionale di Statistica)

2.3 THE RECESSION OF 1992–3

An important factor in this recession was the fall in consumption (2.1 per cent in 1993) following the fall in household disposable income. This drop in consumption started in the second half of 1992 and continued into the first quarter of 1993; it particularly affected the demand for consumer durables, which fell 10.3 per cent in 1993. Expenditure on cars fell a staggering 20.4 per cent in that year. Household consumption continued its decrease during the first nine months of 1993, about 1.8 per cent compared to the corresponding period of 1992, although the rate of the decrease slowed down as 1993 progressed. It was the first time since World War II that household spending in Italy had fallen for five consecutive quarters (Q4 1992 to Q4 1993 inclusive); not even the post-oil-crisis recession of 1974–5 was so deep.

Wage reforms, the fall in employment and higher taxes (VAT was increased from 18 to 19 per cent in the September 1992 budget) compounded stagnant demand by reducing real disposable incomes by about 2.5 per cent (in the first three quarters of 1993). The unusually severe effect this fall in income had on demand can be attributed perhaps to the extreme pessimism of the time. That is, the lower income levels were expected to last for a long time, whereas in the past income decreases had been seen as temporary situations. Perhaps this

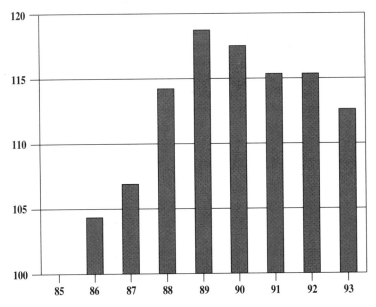

Figure 2.2 Industrial production index
Source: Istat

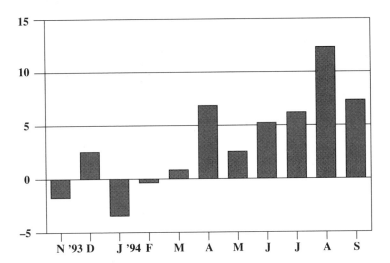

Figure 2.3 Industrial growth rate (%)
Source: Istat

difference in attitude was also due to growing political instability, falling employment and the general economic uncertainty preceding and following on from the currency crisis. The poor consumer confidence continued to affect expenditure in 1993 and continued to swamp the improvements in competitiveness due to the devalued lira until the end of that year. But at the end of 1993, domestic demand started to pick up. It has since led to the sharp increases in growth we have seen in the first half of 1994.

2.4 INVESTMENT ACTIVITIES

As a consequence of the recession, Italian investment has been progressively falling since 1991. It fell in the third quarter of 1993 by 1.8 per cent on the previous quarter and was 9.2 per cent lower than the corresponding period of 1992. The decline was most dramatic in purchases of machinery, office equipment, transport equipment, precision instruments and construction.

In 1992, the main hindrances to investment were the poor expectations of firms and the climate of the recession. This was dampened further by little sign of improvement in consumer confidence, and in recessionary conditions abroad. Other factors deterring investment were the low capacity utilization rates, the high debt of many firms, and high real interest rates. This last factor, however, was somewhat mitigated in 1993. The rate of business closures during the 1992–3 recession in Italy was devastating. A Chamber of Commerce survey showed that closures exceeded start-ups by 41,000 in the first six months of 1993. But the restructuring policies were also partly responsible for this – leading to a gradual fall in the number of small businesses. The fall in nominal interest rates helped to alleviate firms' financial difficulties to some extent, and from Q4 1993 investment started to pick up (Table 2.3).

Table 2.3 Equipment and construction investment and government consumption: percentage change over previous period, seasonally adjusted annual rates

	1993			1994	
	Q2	Q3	Q4	Q1	Q2
Equipment investment	−19.3	−7.5	8.6	13.9	8.0
Construction investment	−6.6	−7.4	−6.0	0.0	0.0
Government consumption	0.4	0.6	−0.1	−4.0	−0.8

Source: Istat

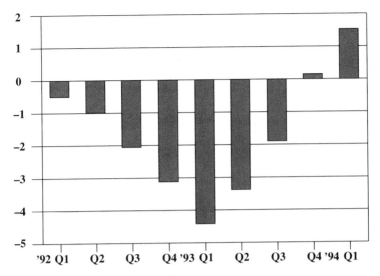

Figure 2.4 Investment growth (%)
Source: Istat

2.5 INDUSTRIAL PRODUCTION

In December 1993, the index of industrial production recorded a seasonally adjusted increase of 1.1 per cent with respect to November 1993, and one of 2.3 per cent compared with a year earlier. Capacity utilization rates remained low all through 1993, and the production of capital goods fell by a further 1.4 per cent between the second and third quarters, although consumer goods recovered slightly (by 0.8 per cent) in response to an increase in foreign orders, showing plenty of room for recovery in the economy. As businesses have depleted stocks and placed more orders, domestic demand has been further boosted. The figures for quarter-on-quarter growth in industrial production show vast improvements of 18.7 per cent growth in Q2, falling to 8.4 per cent in Q3, compared to the second and third quarters of 1993, when industrial production growth was –4.6 per cent and –0.4 per cent, respectively.

2.6 INFLATION IN THE 1990s

In 1993 the average rise in consumer prices was 4.2 per cent, which was below the official target of 4.5 per cent. This was the lowest rate for twenty-five years, and was a significant improvement on the

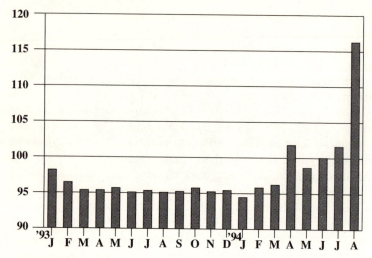

Figure 2.5 Industrial production index, monthly (1993–4)
Source: Confindustria

inflation rate of 5.4 per cent in 1992. The recession contributed to containing domestic inflationary pressures in spite of the depreciation of the lira.

The wage reform measures introduced in July 1992 and July 1993 were instrumental in controlling inflation. These measures included the abolition (in 1992) of the *scala mobile* – i.e. the scheme of linking wage rises to price inflation. The reforms also reinforced the use of incomes policies (introduced in 1993) as an instrument to control inflation. They came at the right time and played a vital role in holding down inflation. Moderate increases in unit labour costs for domestically produced goods and a weak domestic demand also helped to dampen inflationary pressures. The anti-inflationary effects of the government measures have been more fully portrayed in 1994.

Importers' price increases were in fact negligible following the devaluation of the lira in 1992 owing to an effort to keep their market shares during Italy's economic hardship. The large 3 per cent fall in consumer spending triggered an unusual degree of competitive activity at the retail level. Profit margins diminished as shown in the consumer price index data (Tables 2.4 and 2.5). It appears that foreign producers lowered their foreign currency prices in the Italian markets by about 6–8 per cent, thus offsetting some of the depreciation. All these factors acted to rein-in the inflationary effects of the devaluation.

Table 2.4 Consumer prices, producer prices and earnings indices

	1985	1986	1987	1988	1989	1990	1991	1992	1993
Consumer price index	100	106.1	111.0	116.5	124.2	131.8	140.3	147.7	153.9
Producer price index	100	100.2	103.2	106.8	113.1	117.8	121.7	124.0	128.7
Earnings index	100	104.8	111.6	118.4	125.6	134.7	147.9	155.9	161.2

Source: Istat

Table 2.5 Inflation indicators

	1993 Q4	1994 Q1	Q2	Q3
Consumer prices	4.1	4.2	4.0	3.7
Producer prices	3.9	3.5	3.1	na
Earnings	3.8	4.2	4.1	na

Source: Istat

Since 1992, the lira has lost 24 per cent of its value on a trade-weighted basis. Italy imports about 32 per cent of its consumption and investment goods. The rate of inflation has been repressed during the recession, partly owing to the lack of domestic demand. In 1994, nominal wage increases have been in line with increases in consumer prices. Inflation has stabilized at around 4 per cent and in fact the latest figures available at the time of completion of this survey show a fall to 3.6 per cent (August 1994), which is the lowest level since September 1969. The government projects a year-end inflation rate of 3.5 per cent for 1994 and 2.5 per cent for 1995 in its 1995 budget document. The most important element in the falls in inflation so far has been the containment of wage demands; the recession has also played a key role in the past. The unemployment slack in the economy, however, should be more than sufficient to contain this for a long while yet.

There is still a great deal of slack in the economy, with unemployment at 11 per cent. Furthermore there are other criteria reflecting capacity, based on utilization of the economy, which suggest that there is little evidence of inflationary pressure. If the government's inflation targets for 1994 (3.5 per cent) and 1995 (2.5 per cent) are exceeded, wage contracts will have to be adjusted for the excess in the inflation rate. Firms may be forced by trade unions to make concessions. Some large firms were still laying-off workers as recently as May 1994.

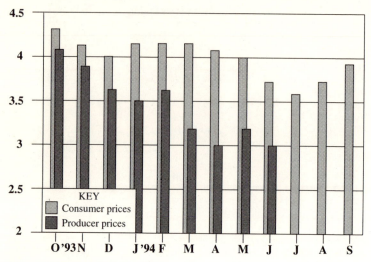

Figure 2.6 Monthly inflation indicators
Source: Istat

2.7 THE LABOUR MARKET

A detailed account of the developments and structural reforms of the
Italian labour market in the 1990s is given later in the study. The
reader is referred to Chapter 3 below.

2.8 THE EXTERNAL BALANCE

Historically Italy's trade deficit has been offset by an invisibles surplus,
but the invisibles balance very much worsened during the 1980s.

2.8.1 The trade balance

The current account in Italy has been mostly in deficit since the 1970s
and 1980s, except for the surplus of the year 1986. The deficit reached
$21.4 bn in 1991 as Italian imports continued to increase whilst export
growth did not catch up. The response of the Italian trade balance to
the devaluation of the lira after the ERM crisis in September 1992 was
very favourable and almost immediate. The trade balance swung into
surplus in 1993 at L51,106 bn. Exports became relatively cheaper,
more competitive. The depreciation counteracted the losses of competitiveness experienced since 1989. The actual nominal depreciation
of the lira in 1993 was about 20 per cent compared to the pre-crisis
level. The trade balance moved into surplus from January 1993, as
shown in Figure 2.8, and continued to improve throughout the rest of

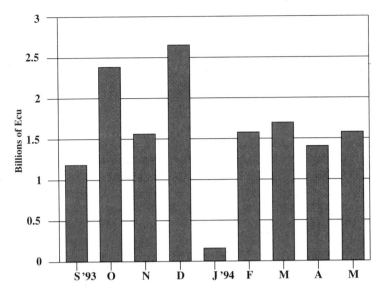

Figure 2.7 Monthly visible trade balance
Source: Istat

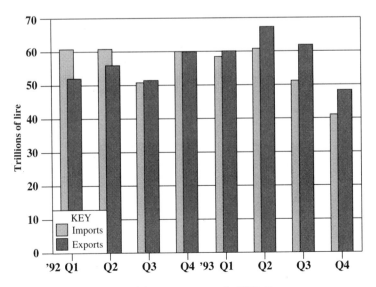

Figure 2.8 Exports and imports, quarterly 1992–3
Source: Istat

the year. This was also in part due to a decline in domestic demand, which contributed to the fall in foreign imports. The current account surplus in 1993 reached L17,985 bn ($11.4 bn).

A number of government initiatives have been taken in 1993–4 to improve Italian export performance. Italy's foreign trade agency (ICE) has been combining forces with regional export consortia to overcome the disparate nature of Italy's export promotion effort. In January–June 1994, Italy's trade surplus with countries outside the European Union was L10,642 bn – more than twice the surplus of L4,221 bn recorded in the corresponding period of 1993. In comparison with the same period in 1993 exports grew by 18.4 per cent in lira terms and imports by just 7.9 per cent. Breakdown by sector reveals growth in all sectors except agriculture and mineral products. Large surpluses were recorded with the USA and the newly industrialized countries of SE Asia to which exports grew by over 40 per cent.

The traditional surplus and positive trend in the invisibles balance has been reversed since the mid-1980s and reached a deficit of $28 bn in 1992. There are two main reasons for this:

- Increased net outgoings on investment income
- and a lower net tourism surplus as Italians spent more abroad (up to $16.5 bn in 1992).

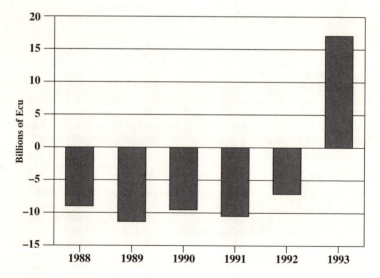

Figure 2.9 Visible trade balance
Source: Istat

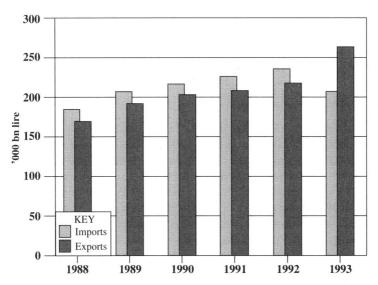

Figure 2.10 Exports and imports 1988–93
Source: Istat

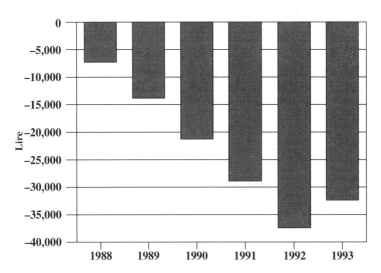

Figure 2.11 Invisibles balance, billions of lire
Source: Istat

The invisibles deficit fell to L33,121 bn ($21 bn) in 1993, owing mainly to a large rise in the net tourism surplus. Also, Italian companies have been investing more abroad in recent years, leading to net outflows on the direct investment and portfolio accounts.

2.8.2 The capital account

The deficits on the current account in 1991 and 1992 were only partly compensated for by capital inflows. Thus, a severe draining of foreign currency reserves has taken place. In 1993 both inflows and outflows of non-bank capital nearly doubled, indicating an important growth in activity perhaps inspired by optimism about the vigour of the Italian economy's progress and future. But after substantial inflows of capital in the early months of 1994, mostly in foreign portfolio investment, growing political uncertainty led to a capital outflow of L4,600 bn in May 1994 and L14,150 bn in June 1994. Over the first half of 1994, therefore, an overall deficit was recorded of L17,147 bn compared to a surplus of L17,449 bn in the same period in 1993.

2.8.3 The behaviour of the lira

In January 1990, the lira entered the ERM narrow band of 2.25 per cent. During 1990 and 1991, strong capital inflows helped push the lira up to near its ceiling against several other ERM currencies including the DM, requiring frequent interventions on the part of the Central Bank – *Banca d'Italia*. The first half of 1992 witnessed a new period of instability – linked to uncertainty about Italy's ability to meet the Maastricht Treaty's convergence criteria for inflation, interest rates and public sector debt. On 8 August 1992 intervention by the Bundesbank and the Bank of Italy was required when the lira fell below its ERM floor of L765.40 (per DM). In September, there was a 7 per cent devaluation of the lira which preceded the withdrawal from the ERM, and then a further drop in the lira: DM rate to L890 followed. By the end of 1992, the rate had fallen to almost L1,000, but by 1993 it returned back towards L900 and by mid-1993 market confidence had been revived by the Ciampi government's programme for the economy. Political instability, both before and after the March 1994 elections, added to the weakness of the lira. The international markets saw the lira fall again in the summer of 1994, dropping to L1,030 in mid-August 1994 in the aftermath of the 0.5 per cent increase in the discount rate by the Bank of Italy. It fell to a low of around L1,037 following the announcement of investigation

Table 2.6a Nominal effective exchange rate index: annual data, 1985–93

1985	1986	1987	1988	1989	1990	1991	1992	1993
100	101.4	101.2	97.8	98.6	100.6	98.9	95.7	79.6

Table 2.6b Nominal effective exchange rate index: 1994 monthly data, December 1993–August 1994

Dec '93	Jan	Feb	Mar	Apr	May	Jun	Jul	Aug
76.1	76.2	76.4	75.9	78.0	78.2	77.1	76.3	75.4

Source: Bank of England
Note: The nominal effective exchange rates are period averages of Bank of England trade-weighted indices

Table 2.7 Real effective intra-EU exchange rates

										1992	
										Nov	*Dec*
										93.8	90.7
				1993							
Jan	*Feb*	*Mar*	*Apr*	*May*	*Jun*	*Jul*	*Aug*	*Sep*	*Oct*	*Nov*	
88.6	87.3	85.1	85.5	89.7	91.1	89.7	89.0	87.5	86.9	86.0	

Source: Banca d'Italia, Economic Bulletin, Number 18, February 1994

of Berlusconi in late November 1994 and has since risen to L1,026, but is at present in mid-December at another low of L1,044.

An economy that has made such considerable strides in lowering inflation and improving the current account balance would normally have an appreciating currency. Yet this adjustment has been hampered by Italy's fiscal and political problems. The lira thus remains unstable.

2.9 MONETARY POLICY

A tough monetary stance in Italy over the past decade has prevented the public sector borrowing requirement (PSBR) from exerting additional inflationary pressures on the economy. The reduced inflation has also been helped by the 1993 incomes policy. In the summer of 1992, the Bank of Italy increased its discount rate from 12 per cent to 15 per cent, to counteract forces building up on the lira and other weak currencies in the ERM. After departure from the ERM, however, the discount rate fell back to 7 per cent, the lowest level in eighteen years.

Table 2.8 Interest rates

	1991	1992	1993	1993 Q4	1994 Q1	1994 Q2	Jun	Jul	Aug	Sept (28th)
Discount rate	11.9	12.8	9.8	8.1	7.8	7.3	7.0	7.0	7.3	7.5
Treasury bills										
3 months	10.6	12.2	10.5	7.6	7.2	6.7	6.9	7.1	7.9	7.8
6 months	10.9	12.5	10.5	7.8	7.4	6.8	6.9	7.3	7.9	8.5
1 year	11.7	13.3	10.7	8.0	7.6	7.1	7.2	7.8	8.4	8.8

Source: Bank of Italy

In August 1994 (as discussed above) the Bank of Italy, for the first time since September 1992, reversed the downward trend in interest rates and increased the discount rate to 7.5 per cent.

Since the collapse of the ERM the Italian government has faced wide exchange rate fluctuations. Avoiding exchange rate-induced inflation has remained its objective. Great attention has been paid to reining-in the money supply. The target range for M2 growth for 1993 was left more or less the same – at about 6 per cent – despite the prospects of greater inflationary pressures due to the lira's devaluation. The yields on the three-month Treasury bill were guided down to more

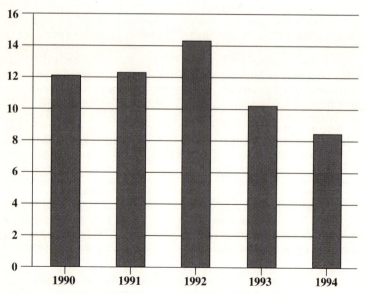

Figure 2.12 Interest rates: three-month Treasury bills
Source: Banca d'Italia

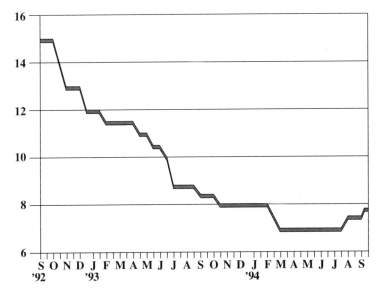

Figure 2.13 Discount rate
Source: Banca d'Italia

Table 2.9 Interest rates – international comparisons, September 1994

	Banks, prime	*Ten-year government bond yields*
Australia	9.50	10.20
Sweden	9.50	10.84
Italy	**9.38**	**11.42**
Belgium	9.25	8.41
Denmark	8.00	8.83
France	7.95	7.99
Spain	7.85	10.77
United States	7.75	7.59
Germany	7.50	7.43
Canada	7.00	8.99
Britain	6.75	8.91
Switzerland	5.38	5.43
Japan	3.00	4.51

Sources: Central Banks of the respective countries
Notes: Interest rates % per annum (27 September 1994)
Government bond yields – ten-year bond rates

sympathetic levels considering the steady lowering of inflation and the fragile state of the economy. At the start of 1993, the better-than-expected rates of inflation and the stabilization initiatives taken by the Ciampi government imbued the markets with confidence, leading to further cuts in official lending rates. This policy was halted, however, when fears of renewed fiscal laxity and political instability led to the exchange rates dropping to record lows. In April 1993, the referendum results and a further easing of monetary policy in Germany allowed further cuts in interest rates. Further decreases followed in May, June, July, September and October.

The persistence of large risk premia in domestic interest rates has reflected fears of further currency depreciation (see Table 2.6). Also, continuing political uncertainties have contributed to this, as yields on Italy's foreign currency issues were substantially higher than those on other currency issues by 50–60 basis points. Interest rates rose 0.35 per cent between June and October 1994, reflecting the perceived risk attached to investment in Italy, and investments denominated in lire.

2.10 FISCAL POLICY

Italy's fiscal problems (discussed in detail in section 2.4 of this study) may take years to correct. The budget proposals presented to Parliament in September 1994 were important for the credibility of the Berlusconi government. The budget aims to cut the 1995 deficit by 48 trillion lire, which would reduce it to under 8 per cent of GDP in 1995. The proposal is to save some 8 trillion lire on the heavy 1995 pensions bill. The savings will be achieved partly through one-off measures such as a freeze on cost-of-living adjustments and partly by increasing the minimum retirement age. Various benefits which keep pensions close to 80 per cent of earnings for most employees will be

Table 2.10 Italy and the key targets for EMU

	Current level	*Requirement for EMU*
Inflation rate (Aug 1994)	3.7	3.6*
Budget deficit**	9.4	3.0
Government debt**	123.58	60.0
Long-term bond yield	12.0	9.8***

Notes: *   No more than 1.5 per cent above the three best performers in the ERM
          ** State sector definition, per cent of GDP, 1994 estimate from the Italian
              Treasury 'Finance Law' for 1995 (Budget)
         *** No more than 2.0 per cent above the three best performers in the ERM

Table 2.11 Economic outlook: summary forecasts (1990 to 1993 actual, 1994 to 1996 projections)

	1990	1991	1992	1993	1994*	1995*	1996*
GDP (% change)	2.0	1.2	0.7	-0.7	2.0–2.1	2.8–3.0	2.9–3.2
Unemployment (%)	11.4	10.9	11.5	10.4	11.0–11.1	10.5–10.7	10.3
Consumer prices (% change year on year)	6.5	6.3	5.2	4.5	3.8–4.0	3.1–3.5	2.75–3.0
Current account (bn lire)	-20,378	-29,337	-34,225	17,985	42,000**	57,000**	67,000**
State sector debt (% of GDP)	91.3	97.9	104.5	108.7	123	125	125

Source: For actual data (1990–3) *Banca d'Italia, Economic Bulletin* (No. 18, Feb. 1994), *The Italian Economy in 1994–6; The CSC Mid-year Forecasts,* Confindustria (June 1994) 1988–93; *Istat,* 1994–7

Notes: Public Sector excludes the State Railways (Ferrovie dello Stato S.p.a.), 'Agenzia per il Mezzogiorno', 'Cassa Depositie Prestiti' and INPS (National Social Security Institute)

* Projection estimates: European Economics and Financial Centre

** Figures are rounded to the nearest thousand billion lire

gradually reduced. The other target for spending cuts was health care. Unions have been enraged by the pension cuts; their criticisms have been that there is too much emphasis on spending cuts and too little on raising revenues. Cooperation between unions and government is fundamental to inflation control. Berlusconi's election promise was of no tax increases and a reduction in unemployment. There has, however, already been a substantial fall in state expenditure, of L9,519 bn between January and July of 1994 compared to the same period of 1993. Nevertheless, a great deal more needs to be done. Great adjustment efforts in the public finances have been made since 1992. The 1993 budget was a watershed, showing a decisive approach to tackling structural fiscal problems. This tight fiscal stance helped the monetary policy measures in bringing inflation in line with the best performing EC countries. An improvement in the primary budget surplus in the state sector equivalent to 1 per cent of GDP occurred in 1993 over 1992. There is a danger that deficits may not remain in line with targets and may bring about further rises in interest rates, and increase the risk premium needed to attract capital compared to other EU countries.

2.11 ECONOMIC OUTLOOK

Table 2.11 shows the economic outlook for Italy for the years 1994–6. The actual indicators covered are: GDP growth (per cent change), the unemployment rate, consumer prices and the current account balance, as well as the magnitude of state debt measured as a percentage of GDP. The table also shows the actual value for these variables for the years 1990–3.

2.12 CONCLUDING REMARKS

Economic policy in Italy in the 1990s has addressed some of the major structural problems of the economy. The implementation of these reforms should to some extent help the convergence process of the economy to enter the European Monetary Union. Fiscal consolidation should be continued vigorously, so that the stabilization and subsequent reduction in the debt to GDP ratio is achieved in due course.

Since investors draw comfort from political stability, a replacement for the coalition government led by Berlusconi would appear inevitable. The changed government could restore confidence as the economic fundamentals remain very strong in Italy.

APPENDIX 2A: BUDGET SUMMARY

Highlights of 1995–7 Budget (Financial Law for 1995). Translated from the Italian Treasury Document (July 1994) *Documento Di Programmazione Economico-Finanziaria Relativo Alla Manovra Di Finanza Pubblica Per Gli Anni 1995–97.*

Summary of budget projections

The target of the government is to secure an additional 48,000 billion lire in 1995 – of this amount the government expects to receive 18,000 billion lire from taxes and the remaining 30,000 billion lire through cuts in expenditure. It is intended that the main reduction of 19,000,000 will come from the National Health Service (NHS) and Social Security System. Greater employment flexibility, hospital closures and a new system of payment for medical services based on the patient's income should account for NHS cuts of the order of 6,700 billion lire. The Treasury requires a cut of 2,500 billion lire from local authorities, and from the Defence Ministry a drop of 1,600 billion lire in military expenditure is needed. The main part of the 12,000 billion lire reduction, however, will come from reforms of the pension system.

The important pension reforms are as follows:

- 40 years of work are required for the pension based on duration of work (as against 35 years today)
- new retirement ages for men and women – 65 for men and 60 for women (as against 60 for men and 55 for women today)
- the cumulative entitlement to pensions to be cut to 1.75 per cent for each year of a worker's salary after the end of 1995, from the current (1994) figure of 2 per cent. This motion was defeated in Parliament on 17 November 1994, and the 2 per cent entitlement remains
- reduction of pensions for widowers and orphans with high incomes.

This new pension system will be applied only after 31 December 1994.

Budget highlights for Italy

I Economic situation in Italy

The Maastricht Treaty suggests that the countries of the EU should have a ratio of public debt to GDP not higher than 60 per cent, in order for economic and monetary integration to take place. However, Italy has a ratio of 123 per cent. The main targets for the Italian government to improve this situation are:

- to get a deficit less than 154,000 billion lire, 9.4 per cent of GDP in 1994
- to obtain a reduction in the deficit of 2 per cent of GDP in 1995 – thus reaching a deficit of 138,600 billion lire, 8 per cent of GDP
- in 1996 the ratio of national debt to GDP should be less than in 1995.

II State structure

The present negative budget situation is partly due to the state structure, which consists of:

- centralized decision-making concerning public expenditure, which tends to cause a lack of awareness in the population of the costs of financing government expenditure
- complex state financing which leads to a great deal of tax evasion
- the presence of public sector in production, which creates monopoly situations.

III Proposals

The main proposals of the government are:

- decentralization (giving more power to regional authorities)
- a new pension system
- a new state financing system (which is simpler and more flexible, and includes a cut in direct taxation).

IV Government objectives

The government's main objectives will be:

- Investment policy (the government has suspended the negotiations of the previous government)
- Greater investment in private firms
- Easy terms of payment of taxes for new farms
- More flexibility for farmers to employ more workers
- Less taxes for farmers employing new workers
- Extension of the financing law for young entrepreneurs
- Closing of the intervention in the south.

V Government targets

The government will try to induce further productive activity within the economy as well as creating new jobs. It will also try to decrease the deficit of the budget with a possible reduction in the interest rate.

- The agreements of 1992 and 1993 kept inflation down; this trend should continue. The inflation rate should decrease from 3.5 per cent in 1994 to 2.5 per cent in 1995 and 2.0 per cent in 1996.
- GDP should increase in 1995 by at least 2.7 per cent and 3 per cent in 1997.
- Employment should increase by 0.4 per cent in 1995 and 0.8 per cent in 1997 and the unemployment rate should decrease from around 11 per cent in 1994 to 9.6 per cent in 1997.

VI Public expenditure and reforms

In 1993 the primary surplus was only temporary, due to only a gradual allocation of investment funds and due to the refunding of IVA (the Italian value added tax). The main features of the proposed reforms to assist with the public accounts balance are as follows:

1 New pension system (1993)
The pension reform of 1993 provides:

- the new limits for the pension age have been raised to 65 for men and 60 for women;
- revaluation based only on the variation of prices;
- increases of the pension schemes based on duration of work:
    an increase in the minimum duration of working life (35 years) an increase in the use of this type of pension due to all the new reforms introduced in the pension system during the first half of the nineties decade.

2 NHS
Measures include:

- increased taxes for every type of service;
- rationalization of the health structures and more responsibility to the regional areas.

3 Local finance
More responsibilities given to regional areas.

4 Public works
Rationalization of expenditure, increased productivity and reduction of the number of employees.

5 International comparison

Italy has on average an economy like those of other European countries. Excluding payments of interest, the public debt to GDP ratio is near to that of France, Germany and the UK.

6 Balance of the public finance for the next three years

The forecast estimates of the Italian economy suggest that wages should develop with inflation and the growth of employment. The estimates consider that:

1 the expenditure for state jobs should increase in line with inflation
2 the interest rate of *BOT* (see page 80) should be around 8 per cent
3 fiscal drag will be limited
4 that the share of excise taxes will remain the same
5 that the share of taxes for local authorities should not change

Expenditure is influenced by many international factors including:

1 indemnity to exporters
2 that Italy should help the countries afflicted by war.

VII Estimates 1995–7

The primary surplus should be positive in 1994, around 0.2 per cent of GDP, but negative in 1995, around 0.9 per cent of GDP.

National demand should rise from 10.5 per cent in 1994 to 11 per cent in 1997.

The public debt will be 127.9 per cent in 1994 to 139.4 per cent of GDP in 1997.

Fiscal pressure should register a change of 1.7 per cent.

Expenditure should fall on the internal product of 35.6 per cent.

This political manoeuvring should produce about 4.5 per cent of GDP and around 86,000 billion lire in 1997 (less public expenditure). Inspections to limit tax evaders should increase the budget by 18,000 billion lire in 1995, plus 5,000 billion lire in 1996, plus 7,000 billion lire in 1997.

The saving on the interest will be 2,000 billion lire in 1995 rising to 8,000 billion lire in 1997.

APPENDIX 2B: SURVEY OF STRUCTURAL CHANGE IN ITALIAN INDUSTRY

The following survey was conducted by Centro Studi Confindustria amongst its member companies on behalf of Swiss Bank Corporation and the European Economics and Financial Centre. The conclusions drawn in the overview section below are those of SBC and the EEFC, and cannot necessarily be attributed to Centro Studi Confindustria.

We would also like to thank Professor Alberto Giovanni, who at the time was chairman of the Council of Experts at the Italian Treasury and is currently Professor of Economics at the University of Columbia, Professor Lorenzo Pecchi, also a member of the Council of Experts, and Dr Paola Casavola of the Bank of Italy for their helpful discussions.

The survey

The sample covered one hundred firms across Italy. These are firms that employ 500 workers or more. The response to the survey was very strong, with some 90 per cent of the questionnaires completed and returned. The respondents to the survey were general managers with responsibility for day-to-day decision-making.

Overview and conclusions

Over the past two years the Italian economy has seen what appear to have been significant structural improvements – leading to serious competitiveness gains and, most importantly, a very impressive process of disinflation. These developments have of course been greatly aided by the recession, which until recently has been firmly embedded in the economy. However, with growth now beginning to resurface, a key issue for the financial markets is whether these gains merely represented cyclical progress as a result of the recession, and are therefore likely to be unwound as growth reasserts itself, or indeed whether we have actually seen major underlying structural improvements which will continue to provide benefits in the period ahead – and hence continue to force forward the disinflation process at work in the economy.

This survey attempts to offer an insight into some of the issues raised here – particularly in the context of labour market rigidities. Overall, the survey offers valuable evidence suggesting that Italy has been seeing genuine underlying improvements in the operation of the economy – but perhaps more importantly both that this should continue in many areas and that there is significant room for further government action to aid this process. Most importantly there seems to be a large degree of support for the full introduction of temporary employment agencies. Overall, it leads us to an increasingly optimistic view of the inflation environment.

Key conclusions of the survey

1 The recent period of recession has allowed Italian industry to make sizeable efficiency gains – with some 67 per cent of firms seeing significant gains and none failing to see some improvement. The most important gains here appear to have resulted from labour shedding, improved efficiency on the work floor and a reduction in administrative overheads.
2 There appears to be substantial scope for further gains to be made – with 58 per cent of respondents seeing significant potential here.
3 There have been some improvements in labour market rigidities over the past two to three years. Importantly, the 1991 Law on Redundancy appears to have led to some improvements here.
4 However, despite this progress there seems to be potential for further improvement, which would aid the efficient management of labour resources. In particular companies see potential in pushing ahead with plans for the introduction of temporary work agencies, the use of fixed-term contracts, further liberalization on firing and redundancy and more flexibility on working practices. The government has stated that it is working on these areas at present and there does appear to be scope for positive developments here in the period.
5 In particular, companies see very strong potential in the full introduction of temporary work agencies. No companies failed to see potential benefits here, whilst 48 per cent suggested that there would be significant benefits.

Other points

6 Companies are very much divided on the precise nature of reform required in the centralized bargaining system – although the room for increased flexibility is generally accepted.
7 The survey suggests that the present government's measures already introduced to foster employment creation are unlikely to affect the companies surveyed to any great extent. However, these measures were primarily aimed at smaller companies who are not represented in the survey sample.

8 Companies also see deregulation in the service sector as being potentially capable of delivering efficiency gains in the economy, particularly related to privatization. This is certainly a longer-term potential source of further improvement in the efficiency of the economy.

9 Lastly, companies were asked whether they see the Authority on Competition leading to improved efficiency. The response here was not particularly encouraging, although this may reflect the fact that the sample consists of larger companies and developments here could be seen to be of more benefit to smaller companies.

Dr J. Hall
Head, European Interest Rate Research
Swiss Bank Corporation

Professor H. M. Scobie
Executive Director
European Economics and Financial Centre

I General labour market rigidities

Question: *Do you feel that the present regulations on firing and redundancy, typology of contracts and demarcation issues are discouraging your company from taking on more labour?*

Table A1 Percentage company response on labour market rigidities

	Not at all	*Only marginally*	*Yes, significantly*
Firing and redundancy	19	59	22
Typology of contracts	7	59	33
Demarcation issues	30	48	22

1 Labour market rigidities clearly remain problematic with respect to labour management, although this is less true in relation to demarcation restrictions – see point 5 below.

2 Moreover, the survey may actually understate the effect of these influences since they are likely to impose themselves to a lesser degree in a period in which demand factors have no doubt restricted hiring intentions anyway – once the recovery in the economy increases the underlying demand for labour concerns may show themselves here to a greater extent.

3   *Firing and redundancy* – legislation on firing and redundancy clearly still restrictive from companies' point of view.
4   *Typology of contracts* – a key focus for companies, and at the centre of the debate today on necessary labour reforms. Relates in particular to lack of room for temporary employment as well as fixed-term and, to a lesser degree, part-time contracts.
5   *Demarcation issues* – relate to the ability of individuals to move across jobs within the same organization. This issue has never been considered significantly problematic in Italy – particularly since firms have been able to compensate for the rigidity on regulation through direct bargaining with unions. The results in the table above show that 48 per cent of the firms surveyed are only marginally discouraged from taking on more labour by the present regulations on demarcation issues, whilst 30 per cent do not feel discouraged at all.

II Improvements in labour market rigidities

Question: *Referring to your company, do you feel that in the last three to four years there have been improvements on these issues?*

Table A2 Percentage company response on labour market improvements

	Not at all	Only marginally	Yes, significantly
Firing and redundancy	11	48	41
Typology of contracts	30	59	11
Demarcation issues	63	33	4

1   Firms do appear to feel that improvements have been achieved over the past three to four years – although this is heavily concentrated in the area of firing and redundancy.
2   *Firing and redundancy* – improvements here no doubt reflect the impact of the 1991 Law of Redundancy. This allowed companies greater freedom to make workers redundant – previously such action required union agreement. It also facilitated this process by making the availability of genuine unemployment benefits a reality, through the Mobilitat. Moreover, it reduced the scope for the use of the Wage Supplementation Fund (*CIG*), which had previously been used to prevent lay-offs by allowing the state to subsidize workers' wages. Over the next few years this scope was

again temporarily increased as the recession took its effect. However, these temporary measures will end in 1995.

3 *Typology of contracts* – there has been very little improvement felt in the area of labour contracts. This is the key area offering opportunity for further improvement. It is true that hiring procedures were liberalized in 1991. Advance placement was carried out through the public sector and employers officially had to recruit from an official list. However, the limited effect felt from the 1991 liberalization probably reflects the fact that companies tended to escape the effects of these restrictions and in reality they tended to impose only some bureaucratic paperwork.

4 *Demarcation* – no improvement. However, this may well reflect the fact that this area has never really been seen as a major constraint.

III Issues on which major reforms are required

Question: *In this question companies were simply asked to indicate any areas where they perceived a need for major reforms.*

1 Companies indicating a need for 'work at interim' and 'temporary work agencies' are really highlighting the same issue – i.e. the provision of a legal framework to allow temporary work agencies to be set up in order to provide companies with labour on a temporary basis. The strength of the response here (34 per cent jointly) indicates the potential for such an initiative to bring real benefits.

2 The second most important area also appears to relate to labour contracts – the need for an increased ability to utilize fixed-term contracts. The use of these contracts is presently allowed under specific circumstances but is heavily regulated both by law and within union agreements. Note: in July 1994 a bill was prepared which deals with fixed-term contracts but is yet to be discussed in Parliament. This bill would facilitate the use of fixed-term contracts, since it abolishes the character of 'exceptionally' that the present regulations require.

3 There continues to be room for improvement on firing and redundancy and flexibility in working practices. The latter covers areas other than demarcation, such as overtime.

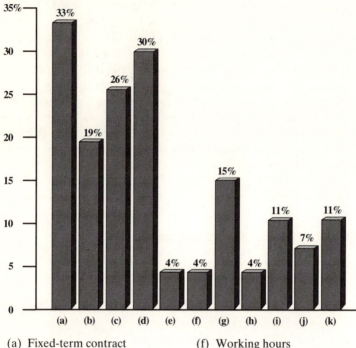

(a) Fixed-term contract
(b) Firing and redundancy
(c) Flexibility in working practices
(d) Work at interim
(e) Employment shares of
    handicapped workers

(f) Working hours
(g) Demarcation issues
(h) Temporary work agencies
(i) Employment subsidies
(j) Part-time contracts
(k) Training

Figure A1 Percentage of companies indicating areas as needing
major reforms

IV Perceived benefits from temporary work agencies

Question: *Do you feel that the planned introduction of temporary
work agencies to allow the use of temporary workers will aid your
company in managing the manning levels in the work force more
flexibly?*

1 The response to this question clearly shows the real benefits
   which companies perceive would be available if temporary work
   agencies were put into place. None of the respondents suggested
   that there would be no benefits – whilst 48 per cent indicated that
   they would see significant benefits accruing from such a move.

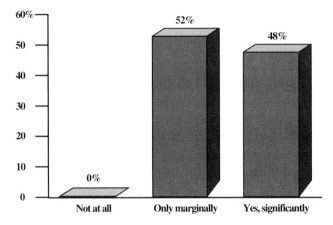

Figure A2 Percentage company response on whether there are benefits from temporary work agencies

2   In the July 1993 labour market accord, it was agreed between the unions, employers and government that this avenue would not be pursued. A final agreement on the precise nature of such agencies is yet to be put together.

3   The main uncertainty relates to whether such agencies should follow the German or British style. In Germany employees are employed full-time by the temporary work agencies, who then pay the employees' wages and allocate them amongst client companies on a temporary basis. Under the British system the companies merely allocate work, with the employees receiving compensation only whilst actually employed.

4   Nevertheless, progress seems entirely possible on the creation of these bodies, and this may well be one issue on which the labour market sees further significant improvement in the period ahead.

V Reform of the wage bargaining process

Question: *Do you feel that a move away from centralized wage bargaining will aid your company in developing a more flexible policy on wages:*

(a)   *by increasing the relevance of wage bargaining at the company level*

(b)   *by substituting centralized wage bargaining with company level one?*

Table A3 Percentage company response on more flexible wage bargaining

	No	To a degree	It would be a major benefit
Case (a)	20	52	28
Case (b)	42	19	38

1   The centralized wage bargaining involves three-way negotiations between Confindustria, the employers' organization, the unions and the government, acting as a mediator.

2   Major steps forward were taken with the suspension in December 1991 and final abolition in July 1992 of the *scala mobile* wage indexation system. Following these moves a new wage bargaining structure was eventually agreed in July 1993. This still heavily relies on a centralized bargaining structure, with only a limited degree of flexibility at the company level. This new system centres on four-year national labour contracts, although wages are set within this framework every two years. Individual companies have some scope to provide additional wage increases – but only related to increases in profitability and productivity. However, the agreements made through this system have been very successful in containing wage inflation – a major factor behind Italy's recent disinflation process.

3   Companies are very much split on the way forward in terms of the wage bargaining system. However, companies do appear to feel that some improvements could be made. Beyond that, the larger proportion appears to favour keeping centralized bargaining, but introducing greater company flexibility within nationally agreed deals – option (a).

VI Effects of recent government measures

Question: *Do you think that recent government measures on labour market reform will encourage your company to take on more labour?* (See Figure A3.)

Question: *From which measures would your company benefit more?* (See Figure A4.)

1   These are the current government's new measures to provide incentives to hire workers and were introduced on 10 June 1994. Decree 331/94 aims at cutting administrative and overhead costs.

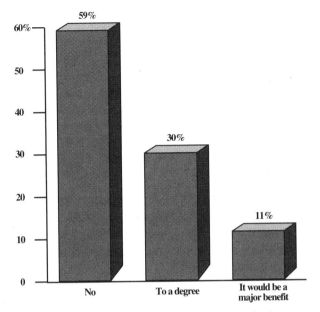

Figure A3 Percentage company response on whether new measures enable more labour to be engaged

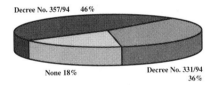

Figure A4 Percentage company response on which measure is more beneficial

Decree 357/94 relates to tax credits for job hiring. Companies may receive a tax credit for two years equivalent to 25 per cent of the income of any worker hired under the scheme on a permanent contract.

2   The survey indicates that these measures are unlikely to have a major impact on hiring practices amongst those firms surveyed. However, the decrees themselves were in fact aimed at small firms rather than the larger employers who were the focus of this survey. This may explain the lack of positive response here.

VII Efficiency gains during recession

Question: *During the period of the recession do you feel that your company has been able to reduce its cost base and improve efficiency?* (See Figure A5.)

1   The response here appears to be clear cut – Italian industry has been able to make significant efficiency gains during the course of the corporate restructuring process which resulted from the recent recession. No companies indicated that they had not seen gains, with 67 per cent indicating that the gains seen were significant. Alongside low wage growth, these efficiency gains were no doubt a major force behind Italy's disinflation process.

2   On the basis of a separate survey conducted by Confindustria on research and development and innovation activity in Italian manufacturing industry, there is evidence that firms have been able to reduce variable costs through the introduction of technological and organizational innovations.

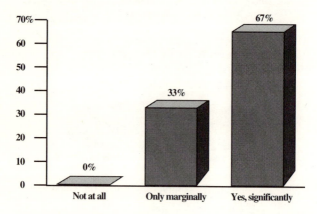

Figure A5 Percentage company response on whether efficiency had improved in the recession

VIII Main sources of efficiency gains

Question: *If so, which areas have been important?* (See Figure A6.)

1   Here the firms surveyed were asked to respond separately to each component of cost reduction and efficiency, indicating whether each had contributed to the efficiency gains seen.

2   The results show clear focuses in the areas responsible for the main efficiency gains. The most important gains here appear to

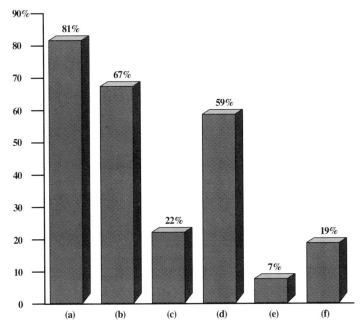

(a) Labour shedding
(b) Efficiency on the workfloor
(c) Re-focus on core business
    activities

(d) Reduction in adminstration
    overheads
(e) Reduction in marketing
    expenditure
(f) Improvements in distribution

Figure A6 Percentage company response on causes of efficiency gains

have resulted from labour shedding (81 per cent of respondents indicating that this area made a contribution to the gains seen), improved efficiency on the work floor (67 per cent) and a reduction in administrative overheads (59 per cent).

3　An important factor here is that the core gains seem to relate more to the control of variable costs. Clearly, it is important that these gains are maintained as production recovers in order for them to be translated into longer-term competitiveness gains – and to keep the disinflation process intact. Question IX addresses this issue.

IX Will efficiency gains continue?

Question: *Do you see potential for improvements in some of these areas to continue?*

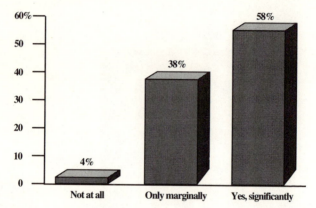

Figure A7 Percentage company response on potential for improvement in the areas

1   There appears to be a substantial degree of confidence amongst companies that further gains can be attained – with only 4 per cent believing that there is no potential for further improvements, and 58 per cent seeing significant potential.
2   At the very least this indicated that the savings on variable costs reported in Question VIII will be maintained.
3   This environment certainly should be a factor aiding continued progress in the disinflation process currently in place in the Italian economy.

X Service sector deregulation and privatization

Question: *Do you see potential for improvements of efficiency and benefits to your company from deregulation in the service sector.*

Question: *Do you feel that privatization of any public companies in these sectors would help?* (See Figure A9.)

1   Companies certainly see good potential benefits from the deregulation of the service sector. Importantly, this may well be forthcoming, and a number of measures are in the pipeline – in particular in the energy and transportation sectors.

2 The majority of these deregulation issues are related to the privatization programme, especially in connection with public utilities, and certainly the firms surveyed feel that the privatization of public companies in the service sector should help significantly.

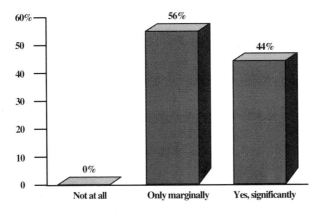

Figure A8 Percentage company response on possible benefits from service sector deregulation

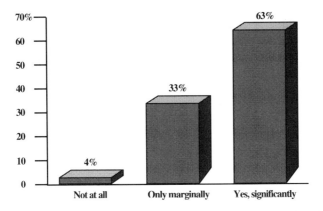

Figure A9 Percentage company response on whether privatization would help in the service sector

XI Improved competition regulation

Question: *Do you feel that improved competition regulation from the Authority on Competition is capable of leading to an improvement in efficiency?*

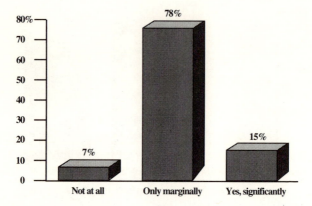

Figure A10 Percentage company response on whether improved competition regulation would help

1   The Competition Law, which was approved at the end of 1990 (Law 287/1990), led to the creation of the Authority on Competition – the official regulatory body in Italy.

2   However, the survey respondents do not appear to consider the activity of this Anti-Trust Agency over recent years as having been particularly relevant to improvements in efficiency.

3   Once again it should be noted that the sample of respondent companies is very much made up of larger companies – and of course smaller companies may feel that there is more potential in this area.

3 The labour market

3.1 BACKGROUND AND CHARACTERISTICS

The Italian labour market has been traditionally constrained by its inherent rigidity and overburdened with state legislation. Indeed it has been one of the most protected in post-war Europe. The regulatory environment in Italy made the hiring and firing of workers very difficult. There have been restrictions on part-time contracts, private temporary work agencies were illegal, and high benefits reduced active job search incentives. These structural inflexibilities were compounded by high state ownership in the white-collar sector.

The principal factors that had affected the labour market included indexed wages, restrictive employment rules, government subsidies and transfer payments to the corporate sector. The supply price of labour remained high in Italy due to lenient benefit systems. Layoff and recruitment restrictions were until recently regarded as the most inflexible in Europe. In principle, centralized wage bargaining does not reflect differences in labour productivity across regions. In Italy it has very much contributed to the rigidity of wage differentials. Similarly significant government cash injections to a number of

Table 3.1 Distribution of employed labour, by sector

Sector	1993		1992	
	Persons (mill.)	Share %	Persons (mill.)	Share %
Agriculture	1.508	7.38	1.749	8.15
Industry	6.736	32.98	6.851	31.93
Other	12.183	59.64	12.859	59.92
Total	20.427	100.00	21.459	100.00

Source: Istat

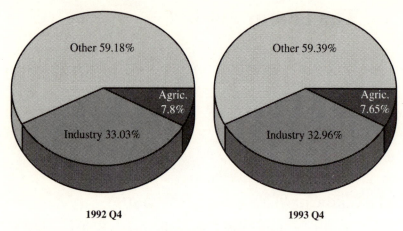

Figure 3.1 Distribution of employment by sector, 1992 and 1993
Note: Due to the change in methodology and data collection of labour statistics from October 1992, figures for Q4 are shown

firms and households prevented competitive downward pressure on wages. The elimination of this rigidity has been the focus of numerous reforms in Italy during the 1980s and 1990s. A series of measures have been introduced that have reduced the rigidities in this market and somewhat eased the conditions for 'hiring and firing'. In this section we shall also examine the recent structural changes in the Italian labour market which have taken place in the 1990s.

3.1.1 Regional disparities

One of the most persistent structural problems facing Italy is the regional differences in unemployment. By 1991 the official unemployment rate in the south was almost 20 per cent, compared to 10 per cent at the end of the 1970s. There has not been much improvement in these disparities since the recovery started, in fact between January and April of 1994, whilst unemployment in the north fell, in the south it increased, showing a worsening of the regional divide. Regional differentials in unemployment in Italy are quite pronounced. And even in recent years the decline in the employed labour force has been much more visible in the south than in the rest of the country. The unemployment rate on 30 April 1994 stood at 6.90 per cent in the north, 9.42 per cent in the centre and 20.10 per cent in the south (*Istat*).

Looking at the Italian economy region by region it is possible to confirm the wide divergence between the north and the south of the peninsula. In the north, there is a prevalence of small and medium firms, e.g. in Veneto (north-east), which operates as a family management unit. These firms create a good grounding for the growth of the economy and manage to create a low unemployment rate of around 4.5 per cent in that region. The area of Emilia Romagna (north) is also healthy with an unemployment rate around 5 per cent. In the Lombardia region (north-west) the industrial system is growing, especially in textiles, with a consequent increase in the number of employed people, 31,000, and a decrease in the unemployment rate from 6.8 per cent to 6.1 per cent. The other region of the north, Piedmont (north-west), presents a particular case. The area around Turin with the crisis in the car sector has an unemployment rate around 13 per cent, while the other parts of the region present an unemployment rate of almost half that. In the centre of Italy, in the regions of Marche, Toscana and Umbria, the economy has been improving during 1993 and 1994 owing to the depreciation of the lira, which helped Italian exports. The unemployment rate is around 7 per cent, 8 per cent and 10 per cent, respectively, and the future seems positive. For the other regions of the centre, Lazio and Molise, the situation is not so good, because they do not have exports and government subsidies have ended. Thus the unemployment rate is higher than 10 per cent. For the south of Italy the unemployment rate is quite high, around 20 per cent. This is caused mainly by the crisis in the construction industry. Sicily, Calabria and Campania (south-west) have an unemployment rate of 22.3 per cent, 23.13 per cent and 23.18 per cent, respectively. For the other regions, Puglia, Basilicata and Sardinia, the rate is lower than 20 per cent.

The differential gap has, nevertheless, somewhat narrowed between 1992 and 1994, mainly because the north and the centre are more sensitive to cyclical fluctuations in the economy than the south. The government's policy for reducing the regional differentials has been to provide funds for training programmes in the hardest-hit areas in the south. The glaring difference in labour force conditions in the respective regions is chiefly due to specialization in, and concentration of, different economic activities. For instance, the south of Italy is very dependent on agriculture, whereas the north and the centre specialize in industrial activities. Employment in agriculture has continued its trend downwards which has meant that the south has continued to suffer from significantly lower employment than the north.

3.1.2 Wage trends

For much of the 1980s the lack of an incomes policy and the auto-matic partial indexation of wages to prices, the *scala mobile*, were the major contributors to persistent wage inflation. Most agreements regarding pay settlement were negotiated at industry or at national level and there was, therefore, quite centralized bargaining. How-ever, the lack of stringent targets made the system inflationary. High levels of state-ownership and large government subsidies also distorted the market, enabling firms to award large pay rises which the private sector had to equal in order to attract labour.

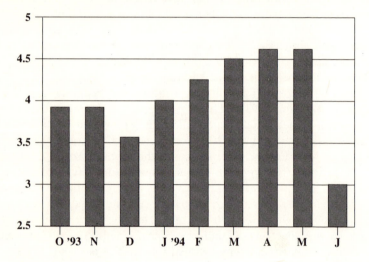

Figure 3.2 Industry wage growth, 1993–4

The *scala mobile*, the system of indexation which started after World War II and was revamped in 1975, was particularly inflation-ary. While negotiations were done at industry level, and were enforced by law for all workers in the sector, they were supplemented by firm-level bargaining. Thus 'leapfrogging' continued and employ-ment decisions were not internalized. The *scala mobile* was officially abolished in July 1992 (although the last actual payment was made in November 1991). Wages were no longer indexed, and the agreement was that workers would receive L20,000 per month over 1993, which was much less than the *scala mobile* increments.

This phasing out of the *scala mobile* was fundamental to the success of the government's economic policy, resulting in nominal wage inflation falling below 5 per cent in 1993. In July 1993, a pact

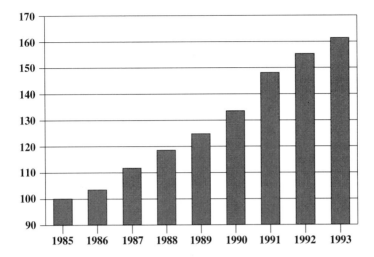

Figure 3.3 Earnings index

on wages and working conditions was agreed upon. It had four main features:

- Wage rises were to be kept within the projected inflation rate.
- Profit- and performance-related pay were allowed by individual companies.
- Biannual meetings were to take place in order to agree on inflation target, GDP and employment objectives between employers, unions and ministers.
- Greater flexibility was to be introduced for starting salaries, as well as the lifting of heavy restrictions on the use of temporary labour.

Currently each industry has a national labour contract determining its minimum wage as well as its salary scales. In all sectors average wages tend to be above the minimum wage, the exception being retail trade and certain subsectors of the service sector, where wages tend to be very low, and thus the average wage tends to be very close to the minimum wage stipulated.

There has been a significant improvement since the wage inflation of 9.6 per cent in 1990. The July pact and previous government reforms showed through into the inflation figures of 1993, bringing the final annual figure for earnings down to 6.5 per cent from 10.8 per cent in 1991. Consumer price inflation for 1993 was also lower than in the two previous years, at 4.2 per cent compared to 6.5 per cent in 1991.

Table 3.2 Wage and price inflation (per cent)

	1991	1992	1993	
Earnings	10.8	7.1	6.5	
Consumer price inflation	6.5	5.4	4.2	

	1993 Q4	Q1	1994 Q2	Q3
Earnings	3.8	4.2	4.1	na
Consumer prices	4.1	4.2	4.0	3.7
Producer prices	3.9	3.5	3.1	na

Source: Istat
Note: Quarterly figures at annualized rate

3.2 MAIN FEATURES OF STRUCTURAL CHANGE IN THE LABOUR MARKET

Italy has had one of the most protected labour market environments in the whole of the OECD. From the beginning of the 1990s the following changes were introduced:

- the removal of barriers *vis-à-vis* hiring regulations. From 1991 firms can autonomously decide whom to hire
- the establishment of an insurance system for the purpose of mass redundancy
- the revamping of the old and introduction of a substantially improved wage bargaining scheme
- the abolition of the wage indexation system, *scala mobile*, the last payment of which was made in November 1991, though officially it was only abolished in July 1992.

Unit labour cost growth has been reduced quite drastically since 1990; there has even been negative growth in labour costs in the service sector. Meanwhile productivity growth has been rising from 0.4 per cent in 1991 to 2.5 per cent in 1993. This growth has been particularly spectacular in the service sector given a fall of 0.5 per cent in 1991; by 1993 productivity growth was 3.6 per cent. This indicates much improvement in the labour market, and provides a strong basis for rigorous growth; it also shows the determined effort made to tackle wage inflation whilst still increasing productivity.

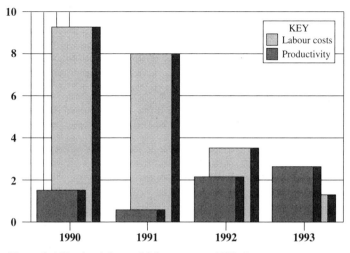

Figure 3.4 Productivity and labour costs, 1990–3

Table 3.3 Productivity and labour cost (percentage growth rates)

	1990	*1991*	*1992*	*1993*
Economy				
Productivity	1.3	0.4	2.1	2.5
Unit labour cost	9.4	8.0	3.5	1.2
Industry				
Productivity	1.6	1.8	4.1	2.8
Unit labour cost	6.8	7.4	2.8	1.6
Services				
Productivity	1.3	–0.5	1.9	3.6
Unit labour cost	6.6	8.8	4.1	–0.1

Source: Istat

3.3 WORKING CONDITIONS AND REGULATORY ENVIRONMENT

3.3.1 Hiring procedures

The hiring system in Italy has been highly regulated, making it difficult to adjust employment in a firm to cyclical changes. Hiring blue-collar workers was done through employment agencies only; the employer was therefore unable to choose a particular worker directly. Attempts at deregulation of the hiring system effectively began in the 1980s and the legislature has been gradually reducing some of these inherent rigidities in this hiring system.

A major part of job placement existed via agencies operating under the Ministry of Labour. Italian labour law meant that those looking for employment had to register with a local office of the Ministry of Labour. Private employment agencies are, in general, prohibited. However, a very small number of such agencies exist in certain sectors (e.g. domestic/home-help workers). For a long period hiring took place mainly via the public employment office; firms could hire directly, but only under the following conditions:

(a) if they wished to hire a worker already employed by another firm;
(b) when certain executive positions had to be filled;
(c) if a firm had fewer than ten employees;
(d) when employment took place as a result of public examinations.

For hiring purposes there was a 'priority list' drawn up by the public employment agency. The proposed candidates were prioritized on the basis of the following facts:

(a) whether the candidate was out of work or holding a job;
(b) the personal circumstances of the candidate, i.e. any dependants.

After a great deal of opposition by firms, these requirements for hiring were eliminated and firms were allowed to hire directly under a law passed in 1991. There remain two restrictions, nevertheless, which involve employers with a workforce of thirty-five or over. They are required:

• to hire disabled workers equivalent to 15 per cent of their staff;
• to hire from the category of 'long-term' unemployed the equivalent 12 per cent of their staff.

Another structural change now under discussion pertains to part-time workers. This would allow more flexibility for a workforce to expand or contract in accordance with cyclical changes. A reduction in working hours or adjustment in wages means that the firms can better maintain a competitive position internationally. Also, greater allowances are being made for flexibility in work schedules.

3.3.2 Labour–management relations

A high quality labour force exists in Italy, with well-educated managerial and supervisory staff available. Managers are not required to include workers' representatives on the boards of directors, but a workers' committee (*consiglio di fabbrica*) is usually set up in order for the workers to be aware of the company's current economic position and future prospects. The mood in the 1990s has been one of dialogue and of compromise. Labour disputes decreased greatly from 35,705,000 hours lost in 1990 to 19,159,000 hours lost in 1992. Unions in Italy tend to be good at controlling their members and negotiating with employers. General civil courts judge on any labour disputes. But the concerted effort to reduce unemployment and inflation taken on behalf of the unions and government together has shown how effective mutual action can be. The present conflict between the government and the unions over the pension reforms in the budget proposals for 1995 are the only area which has caused major conflict, but the government has softened its reforms somewhat in the light of union discontent.

3.3.3 The role of unions

Unions in Italy tend to be influenced by political parties and are organized by industry. All categories of employees are represented by unions. As membership is not compulsory, only around half the total workforce are union members.

There are three major unions: CISL, the centre-right trade union, is associated with the former Christian Democrat Party (DC). (In 1994 a small faction of the former DC party operated under the

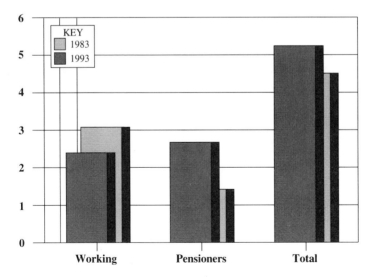

Figure 3.5a Membership of the CGIL, in millions

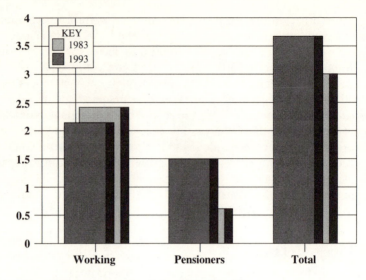

Figure 3.5b Membership of the CISL, in millions

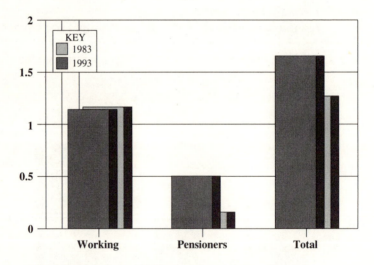

Figure 3.5c Membership of the UIL, in millions

name of Partito Popolare Italiano.) CISL is more a manufacturing-based union. CGIL is a left-wing union and UIL is the centre-left union. There are prospects of unifying all three unions.

Due to their large membership, unions are able to exert a great deal of influence on the economy and, in particular, on the labour market. However, rising unemployment has caused a fall in membership of Italy's three main unions. Two of the three main unions have experienced falling working membership between 1983 and 1993. (The 1994 figures were not available at the time this report was completed.) For instance, the CGIL had 3.1 million working members in 1983. Membership had, however, declined to 2.5 million working members. This decline, nevertheless, has been more than offset by an increase in pensioner members, so that the CGIL was able to increase its total membership over the aforementioned period from 4.5 to 5.2 million.

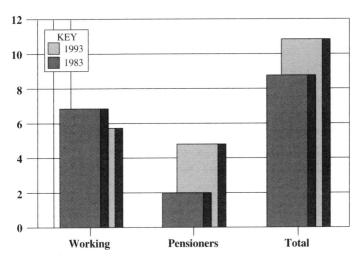

Figure 3.6 Union membership, in millions

3.3.4 Termination of employment

For a firm to adapt effectively to recession and to general cyclical changes in demand, there should be reasonable flexibility in hiring and firing procedures and laws. But the Italian labour market has been labouring under rigid employment and termination of employment procedures. The notice that an employer must give of dismissal varies somewhat according to an employee's seniority as well as their duration of work and the type of work. The minimum notice varies from fifteen days to three months. Without such notice the employer must pay the employee compensation in lieu of the period of notice.

Even if the dismissed employee does not work during the period of notice, the time is included in the computation of length of employment. The compensation in lieu of notice is still payable if an employee dies. Written notice of termination is not required in cases of serious misconduct, but it is often hard to prove that this has occurred. Unfair dismissal (judged by a court) results in an employee's reinstatement or additional compensation. Employers can find termination of employment, especially in disputed cases, very difficult and expensive. All individuals are entitled to compensation on dismissal depending on salary and length of service unless serious misconduct has been proven. Dismissal from work in Italy is controlled by labour–management agreements and by law. Workers' interests are protected by a series of provisions such as notice of dismissal, compulsory consultations, monetary compensation and re-employment rights in cases of a reduction in the number of hours worked.

The Wage Supplementation Fund (discussed below) is also available to companies. The fund thus provides assistance to both workers and employers when companies are forced to temporarily lay off workers, or when they are faced with an economic crisis specific to their area. In addition to the Wage Supplementation Fund there are two other forms of financial help for the unemployed. These are:

(a) ordinary unemployment benefit and
(b) the benefit associated with the *mobilità*.

Ordinary compensation is payable normally for a period of less than three months. However, it is renewable for a maximum of four further three-month periods. When there is a regional or industry-specific crisis, extra compensation is available for one year with the possibility of two- or three-month extensions. Extraordinary payments, though, are only granted to firms with fifteen or fewer employees, six months prior to their request for compensation. When a firm is in the process of restructuring, or reorganization, any extension to the twelve-month compensation must be agreed upon by an interministerial decree. Unions must be informed of any projected job terminations (Law 223/1991) in writing, and the terms should be agreed by both parties.

3.3.5 Wage Supplementation Fund

The Wage Supplementation Fund, or *Cassa Integrazione Guadagni* (*CIG*), is a compensation scheme that allows temporarily laid-off workers to claim sometimes up to 80 per cent of their gross wages.

The *CIG* is divided into two categories, ordinary and extraordinary payments. Ordinary payments are associated with short-term layoffs – e.g. one week – and extraordinary payments are for longer-term layoffs – up to two years or more. In practice, though, workers have been able to claim benefits for years and employers use the system to dismiss workers without much fuss since workers are guaranteed a 'wage' close to their work pay anyway. The *CIG* has been typical of the rigid nature of the Italian labour market – the system clearly acts as a barrier to worker incentives to get jobs, since workers are not encouraged to look for employment as long as firms keep their wages high. Although the ordinary payments provide an essential means to engage firms and workers to cope with adverse periods, the extraordinary payments have been detrimental to the labour market. The regulatory authorities could introduce a benefit scheme similar to those of other comparable nations without reducing the welfare of workers or employers.

In response to rapid output growth towards the end of the 1980s, the number of jobs rose by 1 per cent in 1990. However, the recession of the early 1990s brought about a fall in recruitment, especially in manufacturing. As a result there was an increased reliance on the Wage Supplementation Fund after seven years of declining payments. In fact, the unemployment rate in Italy is 11.6 per cent (July 1994) as compared to 9.4 per cent in Britain, 8.4 per cent in Germany and 6 per cent in the USA. Indeed, in recent history the Italian jobless rate has consistently been well above the OECD average.

When workers are obliged to stop activity or reduce their working hours, compensation is payable out of the Wage Supplementation Fund under three conditions:

(a) Temporary unavoidable adverse events.
(b) Detrimental labour market forces.
(c) Employer re-organization.

When (a) or (b) arises compensation takes the form of 80 per cent of full wage or salary, payable only to workers. All employees benefit from payments when (c) arises, except for executives.

The *CIG* has not been beneficial to the economy, and this has been recognized by the introduction of the Mobility List in July 1991 (see below). The high alternative wage the *CIG* offers makes laid-off workers reluctant to actively look for work and to accept job offers.

3.3.6 Retirement

The budget proposals for 1995 increased the retirement age for men and women by five years; this has caused much union upset, culminating in a four-hour general strike on 14 October and an eight-hour strike planned for 2 December. The Berlusconi government has provisionally made some changes to the pension reforms in response to union grievances. Although the law and the employment agreements may specify the age at which employees are eligible for a pension (60 for men, 55 for women) these are not automatic retirement ages. These limits are scheduled to rise to 65 and 60, respectively, in the near future in an attempt to limit growing pensions payments. An employer intending to retire an employee upon reaching the specified age must give appropriate advance notice of termination of service or pay the due compensation. The pensions reforms have also limited the annual re-evaluation of pensions to the consumer price index alone and not above it. There were also other changes in the calculation of pensions.

Until September 1994 the number of pensioners in Italy stood at the 20 million mark. This means that over a third of the government's total annual spending is needed to meet these costs alone. Given Berlusconi's administration election promises to remedy Italy's public finance problem, the October 1994 budget has suggested pension freezes which would greatly reduce the government's pension expenditure. In the first nine months of 1994, some 460,000 people lodged formal applications for early retirement – a figure which is almost twice that of 1993. This flurry of activity had been brought about by forecasts suggesting that the 1995 budget would contain deficit cuts of some L45,000 bn, of which around one-fifth (L9,000 bn) is estimated to come directly from pensions expenditure. In the event the 1995 budget proposals contained a target to find L48,000 bn.

The pension proposals are:

- The minimum working life needed before one is eligible for a state pension has been increased from 35 to 40 years.
- New limits for the retirement age – 65 for men and 60 for women (as against 60 for men and 55 for women today).
- Reduction to 1.75 per cent for the indexation of the pension after the year 1995, while for the years until 1994 the revaluation index is 2 per cent; this was revoked by Parliament on 17 November 1994.
- Reduction of the pensions for widowers and orphans with a high income.

This new pension system will be applied only after 31 December 1994.

In some industries, such as banking, an unusual scheme has been implemented which provides that if a senior employee retires, then the organization will be prepared to hire his/her son/daughter. Between January and June 1994, 280 people retired from the Carical (*Cassa di Risparmio di Calabria e Lucania*) in favour of their children.

3.3.7 Working environment within private industry

Italy's private sector can be described as dynamic, despite the high levels of taxation and employment regulation. Strict employment laws lead firms to maintain small staff, with much contracting-out and much use of freelances. For example: Naples which, while the centre of the glove industry, does not have one registered glove manufacturer. Firms elsewhere in Italy subcontract work to mainly self-employed women who work from their homes in the Naples region. These small firms and freelances can avoid regulation. Small firms form the backbone of the Italian economy: 1 per cent of Italian industrial firms have over 500 workers whereas 90 per cent have under 100 workers. Abiding by the employment laws and *scala mobile* would have wiped out whole industries.

The 'industrial district' is the foundation of Italy's small-firm economy. In the north of the country, there are groups of small firms that serve the same industry and are based in the same geographical area; such firms are able to benefit from economies of scale. The International Institute for Labour Studies – a branch of the ILO – has described these 'industrial districts' as the way forward for small firms, as opposed to the alternative of assisting them with tax cuts and deregulation. The latter method of encouraging small firms, however, can be detrimental to them in the long run as it could hinder them from employing high quality workers, and can also discourage the purchasing of capital goods which would raise productivity substantially. Though such small firms benefit from pooling their resources, there are two major problems which often affect them:

- Firstly, being small and mostly run by families, they are often short of managerial skills; and the result of this is that they are often devoid of an injection of new and fresh ideas.
- Secondly, their small size prevents them from having easy access to investment capital, thereby ensuring that very few of such

companies are able to expand and make the transition to becoming large companies.

The nature of private industry has to a large extent been affected by the amount of regulation in the labour market. Labour costs have been very high, as hiring and firing is costly in terms of money, time and administration costs. The dominance of small firms in the Italian economy can be seen as a consequence of this abundance of regulation, and therefore, as it falls away under the new reforms, costs will be lowered, encouraging firms with larger workforces to survive better.

3.4 UNEMPLOYMENT – PATTERNS AND TRENDS

Total employment fell to its lowest level since 1972, decreasing by 0.6 per cent in 1992, and by 2.8 per cent in 1993 (i.e. 650,000 full-time workers, new definition). Much of the core unemployment in Italy has been due to labour market rigidities and regional imbalances which have helped to maintain, if not widen, the mismatch between labour supply and demand.

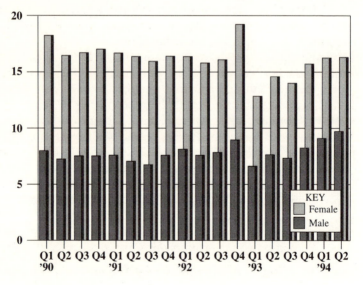

Figure 3.7 Male and female unemployment rates, quarterly 1990–4

Changes in the computational methodology of calculating labour statistics were introduced in 1992 (and became effective with respect to the fourth quarter). Methodological amendments included an extension of the list of branches of economic activity and a redefinition of the term 'job-seekers' that showed a much lower unemployment rate for the third quarter of 1992 (9.6 per cent), the first quarter to which the definition was applied. According to the new definition, unemployment then rose to 10.5 per cent in the second quarter of 1993. The average unemployment rate for 1993 was 10.4 per cent (based on the new definition) compared to 13.7 per cent using the old definition. The new technique of labour statistics compilation was instigated by the European Commission and resulted in the fact that accurate comparison with previous surveys was difficult but, given this, the size of the drop in employment and the rise in *CIG* payments prove that there was a definite deterioration in the labour market situation at the time of the recession of 1992–3. Adding employees who were supported by the *CIG* to the new definition of unemployment raises the rate of labour market slack to 12 per cent in July 1993.

Table 3.4 Unemployment trends – Italy, 1988–93

	1989	*1990*	*1991*	*1992**	*1993**
Civilian labour force	23,870	23,926	24,257	24,257	22,787
Employed force	21,004	21,304	21,592	21,459	20,427
Unemployment as a % of labour force	12	11	10.9	11.5	10.4

Sources: Istat, Annuario Statistico Italiano; Indicatori Mensili; Bollettino Mensile di Statistica
Note: *The change in definition in the computational method for unemployment from 1992 to 1993 should be noted

Indeed the unemployment rate in Italy at the peak of every business cycle since the 1960s has exhibited an upward trend from 5.5 per cent at the end of the 1960s rising to 10.3 per cent in 1990 and reaching 11 per cent by August 1994.

- In 1990 the difference in unemployment rates in the south and the north of Italy was nearly 15 per cent. The gap was more pronounced for unemployed women compared to men.
- Youth unemployment plunged to 39.2 per cent of unemployment in the first half of 1994 due to special unemployment measures subsidizing youth unemployment.

- The structural employment differential between men and women has improved in the 1990s, with 7.4 per cent of men unemployed as opposed to 16.7 per cent of women in 1991, but with the respective figures being 9.8 per cent and 16 per cent in Q2 1994.
- The rebound in measured productivity, obtained through the reduction in employment from the recession, started in 1992–3. This helped to reduce unit labour costs, which fell by 0.5 of a percentage point in the first three quarters of 1993.
- Worsening job prospects in the recession meant that even though the labour force decreased in 1992, unemployment still rose. By April 1994 the unemployment rate had reached 11.6 per cent.

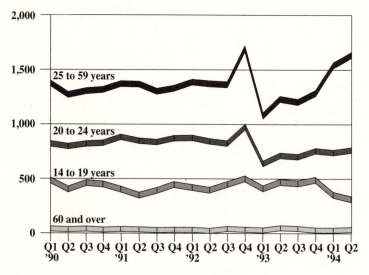

Figure 3.8 Unemployment distribution by age
Source: OECD Labour Force Statistics 1994

To cope with the recession of 1992–3, companies with large work-forces of 500 or more slimmed down their staff during 1993. Job losses were among both white- and blue-collar workers. The contributions made by *CIG* rose substantially, particularly in the first half – by 25 per cent in January to August 1993 over the same period in 1992. The service sector did not escape the shedding of labour after a highly successful period (1990–2) in which the share of services in all employment rose to almost 60 per cent. While the service sector including the self-employed was squeezed severely, the financial sector continued adding to their workforce.

Though the labour force shrank in 1992, the unemployment rate nevertheless increased by 2 per cent to 13.1 per cent between the first and fourth quarters of 1992. In October 1992 *Istat* introduced a methodology that applied a new definition to the labour force. According to the EC Annual Economic Report 1994 the job losses in Italy in 1993 were approximately 600,000, of which almost a half were in services and a third in manufacturing. The unemployment rate, according to the national definition, rose from 9.4 to 11.3 per cent between January and October 1993.

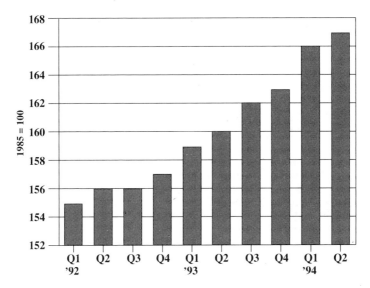

Figure 3.9 Hourly wage rate index for industry

There is confirmation of the success of the wage moderation policy initiated by the abolition of the wage indexation system in 1991, 1992 and continued by the Income Policy Agreement of July 1993. This is manifested by the modest rise in wages of only 3 per cent in the eleven months to June 1994 as compared with a year earlier.

Credit for the moderation in nominal wages can be given to the Incomes Policy Accord of July 1992 as well as the government's suspension of public sector contracts until January 1994. However, there has been a rise in nominal wage growth during the first quarter of 1994 in industry, because some increases were agreed upon under old wage contracts. For the economy as a whole, gross earnings per full-time equivalent worker rose by 3.1 per cent, with a further slow-down that exceeded that in consumer prices. As a result the fall in real terms increased from 0.2 per cent in 1992 to 1.3 per cent in 1993.

The impressive slow-down in nominal wage growth in the first quarter of 1993 was as a direct result of industry shedding labour as well as a concerted effort to reduce wage growth by the unions. The rise in unit labour costs fell from 7.6 per cent in 1991 to 4.2 per cent in 1992 and to 3 per cent in the first half of 1993. The GDP growth prior to September 1992 was hindered by the fixed exchange rate policy (i.e. the European Exchange Rate Mechanism (ERM)), weak demand and the rise in industrial producer prices. The lira depreciation, however, reversed the nominal wage downward trend, pushing the twelve-month rate up to 4.1 per cent in June 1993.

In industry and construction there has been a rise in nominal wage growth in the last six months of 1993, with unit labour cost rising from –3.5 per cent change on the previous year in July–September to 2.5 per cent in September–December, with wage growth particularly high for the first quarter of 1994. Private sector wage contracts on a national level rose in line with inflation.

Table 3.5 Quarterly pattern of unemployment (% of labour force)

	1990	*1991*	*1992*	*1993**	*1994**
January	12.0	11.3	11.3	9.4	11.3
April	11.0	10.9	10.8	10.5	11.6
July	11.3	10.6	11.0	10.3	11.0
October	11.3	11.0	13.1 (9.6)	11.3	

Source: Istat
Note: * The change in definition in the computational method for unemployment from 1992 to 1993 should be noted

3.5 GOVERNMENT POLICY

Two principal factors have strengthened the government's commitment to labour market reform. Firstly, the recession, which started in 1992, and secondly, increasing competition from abroad. Since the recession has reduced profits, firms have been under pressure to cut employment. Since 1991 one million jobs have been lost. The higher unemployment has also weakened the bargaining position of workers during this period, providing a more hospitable atmosphere to more rigorous labour market measures. Unemployment has also been persistently high at around 11 per cent through the 1990s.

The 1992 and 1993 labour market agreements are regarded as a major breakthrough. They abolished the *scala mobile* (the automatic wage-indexation mechanism) explicitly specifying that nominal pay agreements have now to be consistent with inflation targets. The wage indexation mechanism was a system under which wages were set through collective bargaining and were automatically indexed to the inflation rate, so that all wage increases were at least at the level of inflation. This incomes policy enabled labour cost growth to be kept down from 9.4 per cent in 1990 to 1.2 per cent in 1993.

Law 223 of 23 July 1991 provided employees with an alternative to enlisting the *CIG*. The *CIG* gave employees whose hours had been reduced or who had been laid off from large industrial firms the right to claim 80 per cent of their wage for an indefinite period up until retirement. This was particularly relevant to workers laid off during recessionary periods. Individuals could under that system work substantially fewer hours or not at all and gain almost all of their entire previous pay from the state. But the alternative to the *CIG* which was created, the Mobility Procedure, provided income-support measures and government incentives for the re-employment of workers elsewhere. Moreover the Mobility List gave the possibility of a formal rescission of the employment contract. However, the Wage Supplementation Fund and Mobility Procedures were only open to employees of large industrial companies. Therefore, workers in smaller firms and the whole of the service sector were only entitled to ordinary unemployment benefits. This situation was somewhat rectified by bringing employees of the service sector more in line with the rest of the economy by also entitling them to compensation from the *CIG*.

Two years later, Law 236 of July 1993 was an attempt to remove the discriminatory nature of the Mobility List by broadening the scope of its application. Hence, employees made redundant by small firms were also permitted to sign up on the Mobility Lists but without obtaining the pecuniary benefits. By October 1993, 9.2 per cent of the 187,000 people enrolled on the Mobility List were employees from small firms. It should also be noted that the relevant figure for the south alone was 0.6 per cent, showing the inefficiency of the programme in this area.

The July accord: in July 1993 an agreement was reached by the government, employers and trade unions to govern wage negotiations and labour relations spanning the subsequent four years. The prime objective of the accord was to contain wage increases, keeping them below the level of price inflation. At the time of signing the accord it was agreed that this contract would be revised after two years and the terms renegotiated whenever necessary. There would also be biannual meetings to reach a consensus for future targets for the economic growth, price inflation and tolerable levels of unemployment. Wage negotiations will now be more frequent, at two-year intervals. This agreement also made several major breakthroughs. It facilitated hiring procedures by permitting firms to employ temporary workers from temporary work agencies which were to be created. Firms are also permitted to 'rent out' their own employees for a period of time. The number of temporary and part-time contracts increased, largely through the young workers' training contracts which were created. Some steps were also taken for the temporary unemployed by minimizing the delay in payment of their benefit. Although these changes went in the right direction, they did not go far enough. In fact, these reforms were met with stiff union opposition, resulting in large numbers of working days lost through strikes.

Another important feature of the July 1993 accord was the decentralization of wage settlements and the incorporation of productivity wage increases only. The accord permits different increases in the nominal wage rate provided they are related to a particular productivity gain or an achieved improvement in the level of profitability.

The Mobility List, and the July 1993 accord together with all the other labour market reforms have been steadily eroding the rigidities of the Italian system and the inflationary pressures inherent in that system. By allowing wage increases to be kept to government-agreed targets wages have been kept low.

3.6 DEVELOPMENTS IN 1994

3.6.1 Labour relations

Typically industrial relations in Italy have not been entirely smooth. High frequencies of industrial action have taken their toll of productivity, with 35,705,000 hours lost due to disputes in 1990. This figure fell in 1991 and 1992 but rose again in 1993 to 23,798,000 hours lost.

Despite the July 1993 agreement, on many occasions, Mr Berlusconi as well as the Minister of Labour and the task force for employment have held talks with the trade unions and employers (e.g. Fiat Auto, where there has been conflict over redundancies, and Olivetti). Attempts have been made to find alternatives to widespread redundancies but these have almost invariably ended in the adoption of temporary emergency measures which tend to strain public finances. The general strike of 14 October (for four hours) and the one planned for 2 December (for eight hours) are in reply to the stringent pension reforms to help cut government spending – the government plans to

Table 3.6 Labour disputes: man-hours lost

Yearly	1990	1991	1992	1993
Hours lost ('000s)	35,705	19,743	19,159	23,798

Quarterly	Q1	Q2	1993 Q3	Q4	Q1	1994 Q2	Q3
Hours lost ('000s)	5,642	5,477	5,518	5,423	5,294	5,350	5,439

Source: OECD, main economic indicators, November 1994.

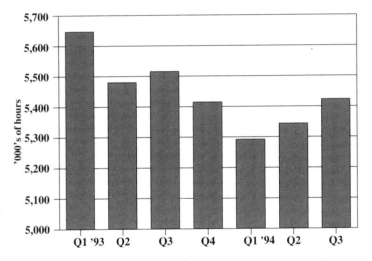

Figure 3.10 Hours lost through labour disputes, quarterly 1993–4

raise L8,000 bn through cuts in pension benefits. On 17 November some of the pension amendments were vetoed in Parliament, resulting in the cumulative entitlement to pensions for each year being prevented from being lowered from 2 per cent to 1.75 per cent. The union action has been seen to be effective in softening the government's tough policy proposals for the 1995 budget.

3.6.2 Decrees

A decree of 8 January 1994 allocated L1,600 bn in 1994 and L4,200 bn in 1995–6 to alleviate unemployment, which had soared to 11.3

per cent in December 1993. The money was used to address problems in the steel industry and Alitalia through:

• early retirement schemes
• and exemptions from social security contributions for three years

There was also modification of the *CIG* in the form of an extension to small service businesses and reductions in social security contributions for companies which reduced working hours. Also if a firm hired new workers on a permanent basis that were previously unemployed, were handicapped or were youths employed for the first time, the firm could have a refund of 26 per cent of the salary of such workers.

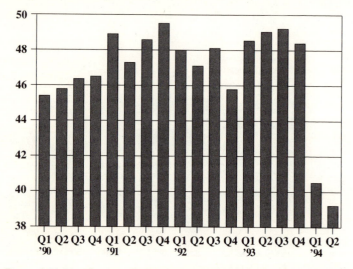

Figure 3.11 Youth unemployment (14–25 years) % of total unemployment

The measures were not over-ambitious but did encourage greater flexibility for employers to a certain extent. Italy's youth unemployment did plunge in response to these policies in the first and second quarters of 1994 to 39.2 per cent of total unemployment in Q2. There has not, however, been much evidence of these policies working to reduce unemployment as a whole.

In the face of this rising unemployment in the first half of 1994 (Q1 unemployment was 11.3 per cent and rose to 11.6 per cent in Q2), Berlusconi's government took certain actions in June 1994 to enhance employment through a combination of tax allowances and removal of some barriers to encourage both youth employment and temporary workers. The reforms contain:

- an element of reduction in the minimum wage for youth hire as well as policies facilitating part-time employment;
- to alleviate unemployment further, tax exemptions were introduced for entrepreneurs up to the age of 30 who were previously unemployed and had set up their own company. The companies are now exempt from all taxes for their first six months in business;
- the extension of the direct hire rules: whereas previously firms with only three employees were able to recruit staff directly, this has been extended to firms with fifteen (or fewer) employees;
- A great deal of effort has gone into freeing-up funds that were previously blocked by the bureaucracy in Italy. For instance, a decree to allow payment of the regional development grants to businesses in the south worth L2,000 bn;
- A three-year package of L500 bn worth of incentives has been introduced to enhance youth employment. This comprises L100 bn in 1994, L200 bn in 1995 and L200 bn in 1996.

Berlusconi hopes to generate 300,000 jobs in 1994. The Bank of Italy believes the measures will at best create 350,000 jobs within the private sector over three years.

3.6.3 Pension reform in the budget for 1995

The budget proposals for 1995 have hit pensions hard. The government plans to raise L8,000 bn through cuts in pension benefits. The budget target is to hold the public-sector deficit down to L138,000 bn (£55 bn), equivalent to 8 per cent of the GDP. The main part of the plan is to increase retirement age by five years to 65 for men and 60 for women, in an effort to decrease projected future pension payments which would have increased steeply with Italy's rapidly ageing population.

The general strike of 14 October 1994 has been a quite powerful instrument in forcing the government to soften its pension reform; talks between the government and the unions are still continuing and final decisions have not been reached. Opposition forces on 17 November joined forces with the Northern League, part of Berlusconi's coalition, to defeat the pensions reforms in the elected house of the Italian Parliament. The defeated measure would have cut the cumulative entitlement to pensions to 1.75 per cent for each year of a worker's salary from 2 per cent starting in 1996. The harsh budget for 1995 has angered the unions greatly, and the industrial action planned seems to have encouraged the government to back down somewhat on its tough plans.

3.7 CONCLUDING REMARKS

The reforms of the labour market in the early 1990s have gone a long way to addressing the long-standing Italian problem of high nominal wage inflation. The July 1993 Labour Accord has initiated a much more coordinated system of wage bargaining which has dampened the persistent upward trend in wage inflation seen in recent decades. However, labour market distortions translating themselves into double-digit unemployment figures still remain a problem. Job losses have tailed off somewhat: in large companies average hours worked per employee have increased considerably, which shows that, as the recovery of 1993–4 is working through the economy, suffice it to say that, while the structural reforms introduced so far are commendable, further measures to make the labour market more flexible would bring it more in line with the rest of the EC countries.

4 Public debt

4.1 ORIGINS OF THE DEBT

The origins of Italy's mountain of public debt date back to the 1970s. In that period Italy entered a period of accelerating government expenditure which was not matched by an increase in taxes. Prior to this period, around 80 per cent of government expenditure was compensated by revenues. Thereafter, this ratio was permitted to fall to around 70 per cent. During the twelve years from 1971 to 1983 Italy's public sector borrowing requirement escalated from 8.4 per cent of GDP in 1971 to a peak of 14.3 per cent in 1983 (as shown in Table 4.1).

From 1982, revenues have not lost further ground but they have been unable to cover the rising expenditure. As a consequence the public debt, which stood at 50.5 per cent of GDP in 1971 and 59 per cent in 1980, commenced its unrelenting climb to 119.4 per cent of GDP in 1993, as illustrated in Table 4.1 (with the corresponding state sector debt at 115.9 per cent). In 1989 the public debt, as a percentage of GDP, broke the 100 per cent barrier for the first time. By 1994 the state sector debt, standing at over 123 per cent of GDP, would still not have peaked. Furthermore, it may not peak until 1996. The early 1980s were characterized by supportive policies of the government towards manufacturing industry, which certainly contributed to increasing public spending. It has only been in the latter half of the decade that Italy has really committed herself to reducing her public sector borrowing requirement (PSBR). This has been partly aided by falling oil prices, which have allowed increased taxes on oil products, and partly due to pressure from the Community to conform in the Economic and Monetary Union programme.

Since 1981, the borrowing requirement has consistently exceeded the 10 per cent mark. The PSBR has, however, stabilized somewhat between 12 and 10 per cent of GDP during the period 1986 through to 1994 (as shown in Table 4.1).

Table 4.1 Public debt and the public sector borrowing requirement (as a percentage of GDP)

	Gross public debt	Public sector borrowing requirement
1971	50.5	8.4
1972	56.5	9.6
1973	58.0	10.5
1974	55.6	9.0
1975	63.8	12.9
1976	58.6	10.0
1977	57.8	8.8
1978	62.4	12.4
1979	61.6	10.4
1980	59.0	9.4
1981	61.1	11.2
1982	66.4	13.8
1983	72.0	14.3
1984	77.2	14.1
1985	84.0	13.9
1986	88.4	12.2
1987	92.6	11.6
1988	94.8	11.5
1989	97.8	11.1
1990	100.5	10.9
1991	104.0	10.9
1992	111.3	11.1
1993	119.4	10.6
1994*	127.51*	10.23*

Source: Bank of Italy, Annual Report for 1993 and Relazione Annuale, 1991, various issues.
Note: Public sector borrowing requirement is net of debt settlements
* Estimate as indicated by the Italian Treasury, Finance Law for 1995 (Budget).
The corresponding estimate for the state sector debt is 123.58 per cent

4.2 THE STATE SECTOR VERSUS THE PUBLIC SECTOR

The state sector borrowing requirement is the main reference variable that the Italian government uses when formulating fiscal and budgetary policies. The state sector covers all the transactions of the Treasury, including current, capital and financial transactions. Moreover, it includes the operations of other central government bodies such as the Deposit and Loans Fund (*Cassa Depositi e Prestiti*), which manages the funds of post office accounts, and also the Agency for the Mezzogiorno. In effect, the state sector portrays revenues and payments of state central administration and Treasury operations

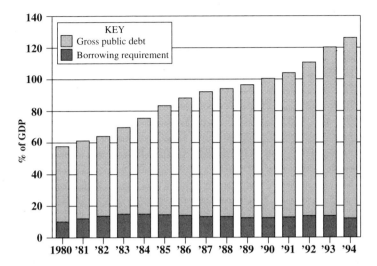

Figure 4.1 Public sector debt and borrowing requirement, 1980–94

including public railways and other public sector firms. The public sector includes all the transactions of the state sector bodies (i.e. the central government and the autonomous government agencies excluding the state railways, state monopolies and telephone company) as well as those of other extra budgetary public entities such as the local government and the social security.

In terms of ratio of GDP, the difference between the state and public debt is a few percentage points. For example in 1993 the state sector debt was 113 per cent of GDP and the public sector debt was 119 per cent. This ratio in 1994 was estimated by the Treasury to be 123.58 per cent for the state sector and 127.5 per cent for the public sector.

4.3 TRENDS IN PUBLIC DEBT

The easing of the public debt burden has long been high on the agenda of Italian governments. Amato, Ciampi and Berlusconi have frequently expressed their commitment to the improvement of the public debt situation. However, up until 1994, in spite of numerous attempts, there has been little headway – primarily due to the short-term nature, and hence the high costs, of the debt.

4.4 PUBLIC EXPENDITURE VERSUS GOVERNMENT REVENUES

Though the fiscal situation for Italy in the 1990s has been getting better, the improvements have not been to the extent the government would have wished. Since 1985 expenditure as a percentage of GDP has increased from 49.4 per cent to its level in 1993 of 55 per cent. During the same period, receipts from tax payments and social security contributions have risen steadily from 1985 when receipts represented 35.2 per cent of GDP in 1986 to 42.9 per cent in 1993 (as shown in Table 4.2). Therefore, although the borrowing requirement has not increased dramatically, there has been little improvement in the debt ratio. Traditionally, the Italian government has been keener to attempt to cut spending rather than risk increasing direct taxes.

On the expenditure side, the running costs for the government rose from their 1992 level of 54.2 per cent to 55 per cent of GDP in 1993. This increase was attributable to several factors. Firstly, interest payments on the country's enormous debts were up from 11.4 per cent to 12 per cent of GDP. Around one-fifth of Italy's government current expenditure comprises interest payments. This also shows Italy's vulnerability to interest rate rises. Moreover, the wage bill for Italy's large public sector workforce rose by 2.3 per cent in the 1993 period, which was higher than the government had planned. Moreover, the deficit of *Insp* (the social security body) was larger than expected due to a rise of 21.4 per cent in recorded claims for invalidity pensions. Subsidies to public sector companies, particularly in the transport sector, were also vastly inflated for the year 1993. These increases in expenditure more than offset any savings that were made in other areas. For example, spending in direct public investment fell by 9 per cent for 1993.

Table 4.2 Expenditure versus receipts (as a percentage of GDP)

	1985	1986	1987	1988	1989	1990	1991	1992	1993
Tax and social security receipts	34.9	35.2	36.0	36.5	38.2	38.7	39.6	41.9	42.9
Total expenditure	49.4	49.6	49.2	49.3	50.4	51.8	52.4	54.2	55.0

Source: Banca d'Italia, Annual Report for 1993

4.5 MOUNTING INTEREST PAYMENTS

Although much of this rise in expenditure can be attributed to the fact that interest payments as a proportion of GDP have risen from 8 per cent in 1984 to 12 per cent in 1993, it is not an area in which the government has a free hand (as shown in Table 4.3). As long as the debt stock remains so high, the debt servicing costs will remain high. This sharp increase in interest payments has in part been accentuated by the devaluation of the lira in September 1992 against foreign currencies in which some of Italy's debt has been held. The Italian Treasury has increasingly issued more debt overseas denominated in foreign currencies in order to gain from lower international interest rates. However, the loss of around 25 per cent of the lira's value has outweighed the benefits of the interest savings at least for a period of time.

Table 4.3 Interest payments and the primary surplus/deficit

	1985	1986	1987	1988	1989	1990	1991	1992	1993
Incl. interest payments	8.0	8.5	7.9	8.1	8.9	9.6	10.2	11.4	12.0
Primary balance	–	–	–	–	–	–0.7	–0.5	0.7	1.2

Source: Banca d'Italia, Annual Report for 1993, May 1994.

Since 1992 there have been primary surpluses and this is expected to increase further in the period 1994–6. As of yet, this has had little effect on the interest payments that must be made. With interest rates across Europe again beginning to rise in the autumn of 1994, the interest payments on Italian floating rate bonds will evidently increase. On top of this all new issues of government securities will have to pay a higher rate of interest. This is of particular importance when one considers the short-term nature of much of Italy's debt. Indeed, by 1993 the average residual life of outstanding debt was 3.29 years, considerably higher than the corresponding figure of 2.5 years for 1990. However, a comparison with other EC countries such as France, where the residual life of government securities was 6.5 years at the end of 1993, shows that Italy is particularly sensitive to changes in interest rates. Although, during the early 1990s the Italian Treasury has begun to favour longer-term notes, in 1994 short-term bills still represent over 20 per cent of all debt. Consequently, when on 11 August 1994 the Italian central bank decided to raise its discount rate from 7 to 7.5 per cent, it effectively increased the cost of servicing Italy's public debt in the first year by 3 trillion lire.

Moreover, the hesitancy of Berlusconi's government *vis-à-vis* public debt and the government's unwillingness to introduce a veritable austerity programme, has led to an increased cost of borrowing for the Italian government compared to other countries such as Germany in the run up to the publication of the 1995 budget. Italian long-term bond rates, which in September 1994 stand at around 12 per cent, are some 470 basis points higher than their German counterparts. This differential has widened substantially since the beginning of 1994, when the gap was nearer 300 basis points. The differential increased in order to attract investment in an environment of fiscal uncertainty.

4.6 THE PRIMARY BALANCE

The public sector borrowing requirement has in fact been reduced from 167.5 trillion lire in 1992 to 164.8 trillion in 1993. This represents a fall of 0.5 per cent of GDP from 11.1 per cent in 1992 to 10.6 per cent in 1993. This reduction in the borrowing requirement in Italy comes as a consequence of an improving primary balance (the balance of revenues and expenditure excluding debt servicing payments). As recently as 1991 this balance was in the red and gave way to surpluses in subsequent years (as shown in Table 4.3). This primary surplus is expected to grow in the years 1994 to 1996 and therefore should ease Italy's public sector borrowing requirement.

It should be noted that the primary surplus in fact improved slightly from 1992 to 1993. In 1992 the primary surplus was equivalent to 0.7 per cent of GDP, which then rose to 1.2 per cent in 1993. Indeed, Italy was the only G7 country to record a primary surplus during 1993, which is a considerable achievement given the recession of that period. However, there are some extraordinary or one-off items which should be considered when judging the success of these figures.

4.7 THE DEBT POSITION IN 1994

The target for the 1994 state sector borrowing requirement was set at 144 trillion lire in September 1993. This, according to the Treasury, was to be achieved by a cut in expenditure of 25.5 trillion lire and an increase in revenues worth 5.5 trillion lire. The majority of the savings in spending were to come from pension and health bill cuts, whereas revenues were to rise due to increased indirect taxes. However, following indications that GDP growth would be less impressive for the year than the over-optimistic predictions (1.3 per cent after the first quarter results of 1994 as opposed to 1.6 per cent estimated in

September 1993), the Treasury issued a revised version to parliament in June 1994 for state sector borrowing of 154 trillion lire (as illustrated in Table 4.4).

The deficit of *Inps* alone, the Italian State Pension body, is estimated to reach 80 trillion lire, which represents over one half of the whole budget deficit for 1994. Even this new figure can only be attained with the suspension of many public investment programmes. In fact, in July 1994 the Treasury Minister, Mr Lamberto Dini, declared that Italy was struggling to keep to this new deficit target. He announced that 5 trillion lire would have to be found to maintain the deficit at the revised 154 trillion lire, or 9.4 per cent of GDP. It remains to be seen whether this amount can be collected through property taxes as Mr Dini's proposal suggests. The plan relies on clearing up the backlog of taxes on properties erected without proper permission through the easing of rigorous tax assessment guidelines that the authorities have to follow.

Table 4.4 The revised projection for the year 1994 (trillion lire)

	State sector (% GDP)	Public sector (% GDP)
Total receipts	520.770 (31.80)	754.787 (46.09)
Total payments (net of interest)	492.970 (30.10)	737.920 (45.06)
Balance of financial operations	−12.070 (0.74)	−9.281 (0.57)
Primary surplus	15.730 (0.96)	7.586 (0.46)
Interest payments	169.730 (10.37)	175.066 (10.67)
Borrowing requirements	154.000 (9.40)	167.480 (10.23)
Gross debt	2,023.584 (123.58)	2,088.029 (127.51)

Source: Finance Law for 1995 (Budget)

Moreover, in June 1994 the government approved a decree that will simplify the tax system, promote investments and generate tax gains during the fiscal years 1994–7 (as shown in Table 4.5). The new measures include eliminating normal taxes for newly founded businesses (set up by the young and the unemployed) and introducing a lump sum payment during the first three years of their establishment. Also, tax credits have been introduced for firms that hire new employees on a permanent basis. Though the Berlusconi government is confident that this package will produce net tax gains of 1.25 trillion lire in 1995 followed by somewhat smaller gains in the next two years, others believe that these gains have been overstated. In any case, the costs of implementing these changes will be negligible.

Table 4.5 Government estimates of tax effects of the June 1994 decree (in billion lire)

	1994	1995	1996	1997
Simplification of the tax system	–	–	–	–
Employment tax credit	124	630	367	236
Investment tax credit	–105	–321	80	–
Flat rate on dividend	–	–	–	–
Tax bonus for newly listed firms	–	–	–	–
Other	–	170	170	170

Source: The Italian Treasury decree of June 1994.

4.8 SETBACKS FOR THE CONTROL OF EXPENDITURE

• Wage agreements: during August 1994, the Transport Minister Publio Fiori agreed on an informal bonus deal for the state railway system's (*Ferrovie Statale*) train drivers. This deal would be worth 70 billion lire for the 20,000 train drivers. If this agreement is extended to the rest of the company then this figure would rise to 400 billion lire. A political precedent has been set which could lead to further demands from other public sector companies.

• Payment of pension arrears: a court ruling of June 1994 found that the government had to pay arrears on certain types of pension dating back to 1983. It was decided that the cost would amount to 32 trillion lire, which should be paid in full during 1995.

4.9 GOVERNMENT BUDGETARY PERFORMANCE

During the fiscal years 1993 and 1994 the accuracy of the initial budget published by the Italian government has been somewhat unreliable (see Table 4.6). In the course of the year the budget comes under close scrutiny and often undergoes several revisions. During both 1993 and 1994 the state sector borrowing requirement was revised upwards and the projected primary surplus was deemed to be unrealistic. The main reason for these realignments was an over-optimistic growth rate projection. For 1993, the budget relied upon an annual growth rate of 0.4 per cent whereas the actual rate was –0.7 per cent. Similarly, during 1994 the GDP growth was lower than expected by 0.3 per cent (1.3 per cent instead of 1.6 per cent).

Table 4.6 Planned versus actual budget indicators (trillion lire)

		1993			1994	
	Target	*Revision**	*Actual*	*Target*	*Revision**	*Actual*
State sector borrowing requirement	150	151.2	153.5	144.2	154.0	–
Primary balance	50	31.5	27.5	31.8	15.7	–

Source: Bank of Italy Reports 1993–4.
Note: * July revision

4.10 PUBLIC DEBT PROSPECTS FOR 1995

4.10.1 The 1995 budget target

The Treasury's target for 1995 is to restrict the state sector borrowing requirement to 138.6 trillion lire and 148.2 trillion lire for the public sector borrowing requirement. These figures represent 8.03 per cent and 8.58 per cent of GDP, respectively (as shown in Table 4.7). This means that the Treasury has to find some 47 trillion lire in a combination of expenditure cuts and revenue increases to give an end result of a 2 per cent reduction in the borrowing requirement as a percentage of GDP. Without intervention on behalf of the government, the Treasury estimates that the state sector borrowing requirement would be as high as 185.6 trillion lire and that of the public sector would be 195.2 trillion lire of expenditure cuts and revenue increases to give an end result of a 2 per cent reduction in the borrowing requirement as a percentage of GDP (see Appendix 2A).

4.10.2 Measures for the control of public expenditure

As mentioned above, the aim of the 1995 budget (details of which can be found in the Appendix to the section on economic perfor-mance, i.e. Appendix 2A) will be to find 47 trillion lire. Of this total,

Table 4.7 The 1995 budget targets

	State sector (% GDP)	Public sector (% GDP)
Total receipts	550.410 (31.88)	796.193 (46.11)
Total payments (net of interest)	511.105 (29.60)	762.255 (44.15)
Balance of financial operations	−5.155 (0.30)	−4.591 (0.27)
Primary surplus	34.150 (1.98)	29.347 (1.70)
Interest payments	172.750 (10.0)	177.539 (10.28)
Borrowing requirements	138.600 (8.03)	148.191 (8.58)
Gross debt	2,145.044 (124.23)	2,219.080 (128.52)

Source: Finance Law for 1995 (Budget)

the Treasury plans to cut 25.8 trillion lire from expenditure. The main features of this saving plan are as follows:

- 8 trillion lire to be cut from pensions. This is to be done by extending the retirement age from 60 to 65 years for men and from 55 to 60 for women. Moreover, from 1995 onwards pensions will increase by 1.75 per cent per annum, whereas, prior to 1994, the revaluation index for pensions had been set at 2 per cent. Therefore, if the inflation rate goes above 2 per cent, pension costs for the government will fall in real terms. Pensions for those widows and orphans who enjoy a high income will also be reduced.
- 6.7 trillion lire to be cut from health care costs. Some categories of the population will now have to pay for their medication. The cut will also involve the closure of certain hospitals.
- 2.5 trillion lire to be cut from local authorities' spending budgets. This is to be achieved through the rationalization of everyday operations in local government. Procedures will be streamlined by reducing the number of levels in the central government bureaucracy.

* 1.6 trillion lire to be cut from defence.
* Hiring for the civil service has been frozen.

When these budget measures were announced in September 1994, they met with stiff opposition from the unions. Indeed, a general strike occurred the following month on 14 October.

The Berlusconi government had intended to create a level playing field for all companies. In the past, some Italian industries or companies have found themselves in a privileged position because they were receiving state hand-outs. The new administration is committed to putting an end to this tradition, and instead will offer advice to companies for improving their operations as opposed to directly giving them financial aid. This move should have a positive effect on both government expenditure and on companies who will be encouraged to become more efficient and productive.

4.10.3 The expansion of revenues

While aiming to cut costs, the 1995 budget also aims to obtain an extra 17.8 trillion lire primarily through raised taxes. The government proposes to achieve this objective through the following measures:

* Increase of indirect taxation, particularly for oil-related products.
* Clearance of the backlog of tax disputes. Tax assessment guidelines have been relaxed – often disputes are settled with less than 10 per cent of the sum in question being paid.
* Payment of property registration taxes. Incentives have been given in the 1995 budget to encourage the proper registration of buildings. This move should generate further revenues.

Moreover, the government is keen to increase the autonomy of local authorities in tax collection and will oversee the formation of an institution for verifying the efficiency of public bodies. The main features of the current system, as in 1994, are as follows:

* Local authorities are very dependent on central government for their funds. They are responsible for raising a very small proportion of the revenue themselves, even though they provide a wide range of services, including the health service. There is therefore a great incentive for local authorities to maximize their finance needs in order to obtain as many funds as possible.
* Local authorities are regulated by national standards, which are not tailored to regional disparities.

- The central government has limited control over the funds that it raises. A large proportion of the funds are distributed to other layers of the public sector. As such, the local authorities have little perception of the costs associated with the funds.

By giving the local authorities more autonomy and responsibility, it is hoped that revenues can be increased through greater efficiency in tax collection and that expenditure can be reduced through a more efficient allocation of funds.

4.10.4 Obstacles facing the 1995 budget

There is already growing scepticism suggesting that the 1995 budget is too optimistic and that targets set cannot be achieved. There are several reasons for such feelings on the budget:

- Interest rates rose by half a percentage point on 11 August 1994 from 7 to 7.5 per cent. The extra cost added to debt servicing was not taken into consideration when the budget was issued in July 1994.
- The income to the government of the two tax amnesties, quoted in the budget, has also come under attack, particularly in light of the cuts in local authority expenditure.
- The budget relies on an optimistic rate of inflation of 2.5 per cent for 1995.

4.11 BUDGET PROJECTIONS FOR 1996 AND 1997

In 1996, the Treasury intends to limit the state sector borrowing requirement to 120.9 trillion lire and that of the public sector to 131.05 trillion lire. The primary surplus generated in 1995 and 1996 is estimated to be sufficient to halt the growth of the state debt in 1995 and the gross public debt in 1996. Therefore from 1996 onwards, providing that a sound primary surplus is maintained, the stock of debt will diminish relative to GDP.

During 1997 it is estimated that Italy's debt position will further improve, with the full extent of the structural reforms in government spending working themselves through the system, creating a primary surplus of some 70 trillion lire (as shown in Table 4.9). This primary surplus will in turn reduce the debt burden to around 126.5 per cent of GDP in 1997.

Table 4.8 Projected state and public sector borrowing requirements for 1996

	State sector	Public sector
Total receipts	575.900	832.550
Total payments (net of interest)	521.500	783.750
Primary surplus	54.400	48.800
Interest payments	175.300	179.850
Borrowing requirements	120.900	131.050
Gross debt as % of GDP	123.520	128.150

Source: Finance Law for 1995 (Budget)

Table 4.9 Projected state and public sector borrowing requirements for 1997

	State sector	Public sector
Total receipts	611.450	876.900
Total payments (net of interest)	533.900	806.350
Primary surplus	77.550	70.550
Interest payments	184.500	188.650
Borrowing requirements	106.950	118.100
Gross debt as % of GDP	121.599	126.550

Source: The Italian Treasury budget projections, June 1994

4.12 BALANCING FISCAL REFORM WITH ECONOMIC RECOVERY

The fact of the matter remains that the Italian government is treading a fine line; on the one hand a too aggressive fiscal programme of higher taxes coupled with public expenditure and investment restraint may damage the speed and success of the economic recovery, but on the other hand a too lenient programme will mean that Italy's enormous stock of debt will continue to grow. Economic ministers are in fact threatening to raise taxes substantially in the 1995 budget if sufficient cuts cannot be found. This perhaps explains the delays in presenting the 1995 budget in its full detail; Berlusconi was elected on the premise that he would create a million new jobs and reduce taxes. Breaking this promise to the electorate would severely dent his popularity. On top of this, there are also political considerations both at a domestic and a European level. Any wavering from her commitment to reducing the public debt will mean that Italy is likely to come under attack from the Community. Moreover, Italy has no desire to be left out of the Economic and Monetary Union programme (see Chapter 6). The challenge for Italy's policy-makers therefore lies in striking a balance acceptable to all parties, namely the electorate, the trade unions, the financial markets and the European Community. One source of funds that can be used to alleviate the debt burden, which until 1994 has had little effect on the public deficit, is capital raised by the government through the privatization of public companies. Money obtained in this way can be utilized to buy back government securities on the secondary market and therefore reduce Italy's debt servicing costs (see Chapter 5 on privatization).

4.13 GOVERNMENT BONDS

The Italian government has raised capital through the bond markets, both on the domestic and on overseas markets. By 1990, Italy represented the third largest government bond market, after the United States and Japan. In fact the Italian market, at that time, was larger in terms of outstanding nominal value than that of Germany and the United Kingdom combined.

During the 1980s and the early 1990s there have been a considerable number of reforms in the Italian bond market. Firstly, structural changes have been made within the bond market to facilitate investment and to create a market similar in its functioning to that of other comparable markets. Additionally, there have been significant changes in the nature of government debt, such as the maturity of bonds, the variety of bonds available and finally the internationalization of government issues. In this section, all these aspects will be treated in turn.

4.14 THE PRIMARY MARKET

The timetable for issues of medium- (*CCT – Certificato di Credito di Tesoro*) and long-term (*BTP – Buono di Tesoro Poliennali*) bonds is published annually by the Italian Treasury. The issues of short-term bonds (*BOT – Buono Ordinario del Tesoro*) are usually finalized at short notice and their precise timing is then relayed to the banks. The calendar of government securities issues specifies the dates by which applications must be sent and when interest payments will be made.

The general public and institutions can place their orders for state bonds in two ways; first, by sending sealed envelopes to the distributors of the bonds, namely banks acting on behalf of the *Banca d'Italia*, or alternatively investors can place their orders via the computerized system. In 1994 the computerized system was only in use for medium- and long-term bonds. It is hoped, however, that its use can be extended to short-term notes (*BOT*). When this computerized system is in full use, the time needed to present the results of the auction sale should be shortened, thus speeding up the final allocation of the bonds. The bids from the two sources are read only after the deadline has closed. Any bids arriving after the deadline are immediately disregarded. Once written applications have been entered onto computer to join the computerized applications, Treasury officials then check the details and sign the document to declare the auction closed. The results are finally made known in the market.

The Treasury uses two types of auction for issuing bonds; a competitive auction for *BOTs* and a marginal auction for medium- and long-term debt issues. These two methods can best be described with the use of examples published by the Italian Treasury, as shown in Appendix 4A.

Prior to the introduction of the auction system it was very difficult to ascertain the actual value of the bond, as the prospective investor could be quoted several different prices from different banks, but be unable to distinguish between the commission charged by the bank and the face value of the bond. The individual banks were in fact distributing the Treasury bonds for the *Banca d'Italia*, charging whatever commission they pleased. Instead of this dubious system, with the new screen-based market bonds were sold using an auction system, whereby the prices of the bonds were set by market forces and the principles of supply and demand, as opposed to being fixed by the Treasury as before. Moreover, there was more transparency of bond prices as banks were no longer able to conceal their commissions.

4.15 THE SECONDARY MARKET

In 1988 a screen-based secondary market (*MTS*) was created so as to modernize the Italian bond market and to render it more efficient. This new system was set up with the aim of getting a more precise method of obtaining up-to-date bond prices. The screen-based system also improved the liquidity of the bond market and trading possibilities, as investors had a more detailed and accurate idea of fluctuations of bonds on the secondary market. Thus the creation of the modern system (*MTS*) greatly benefited the investor.

On 11 September 1992 an Italian futures market (*MIF*) was opened. This development was effectively a response to the success of the

London (LIFFE) and the French (*MATIF*) markets, where trading on the Italian decennial bond was a resounding success. The opening of *MIF* greatly improved the liquidity of the Italian bond market and ensured continued growth of investment in government securities. The Italian government also began publishing a one-year calendar showing information on forthcoming domestic and foreign bond issues.

By 1993, it had become apparent that the *MTS*, though a great improvement on the old system, still needed some refinement to attract further business, particularly from foreign investors. For example, unregulated block trading of Italian government bonds was still taking place on the London market. Consequently, the Treasury Minister and the Bank of Italy took steps to enhance the efficiency of the market. New procedures were introduced to speed up the payment of interest and tax refunds for foreign investors. Delays in the timing of these payments had made it difficult to calculate the exact yield of the state bonds, which therefore discouraged investment from overseas. Yet further encouragement was given to foreign investors through the measures introduced by the ministerial decree of 24 February 1994. One of the most important issues in the decree was a redefinition of the obligations of primary dealers. A new sub-category of primary dealers was set up to deal solely with the allocation of government securities. The range of products and services available on the screen-based market (*MTS*) and the futures market (*MIF*) was also extended. These regulations have had a beneficial effect on trading turnover, which increased from a daily average of 8.3 trillion lire in the last quarter of 1993 to one of 14 trillion lire in the first quarter of 1994. The impact of these measures was to facilitate bond trading in Italy and thus increase the involvement of institutional and foreign investment, as will be seen in later sections. In fact, the *BTP* long-term bond is the third most liquid government bond worldwide after US and Japanese issues.

4.16 THE COMPOSITION OF ITALY'S DEBT

The character of Italy's debt has changed significantly during the past fifteen years. Public debt in Italy during the 1980s was notable for the amount of short-term Treasury bonds issued. In fact, in 1982 the proportion of short-term bonds (*BOT*) of twelve months or less was as high as 60 per cent of all outstanding bonds. In the same year the majority of the remaining bonds were Treasury certificates (*CCT*), which fall into the medium-term category with variable interest payments and maturities of two or three years. During this period the Italian Treasury was limited to issuing short-term notes as its record of controlling inflation was somewhat ineffective. Therefore, investors were not confident enough to invest for longer periods of time. As inflationary pressures waned, the Treasury attempted to lengthen the average life of Italy's debt, with the objective of reducing its sensitivity to changes in interest rates and to minimize the costs of issues. The year 1986 saw the introduction of long-term bonds (*BTP*) with fixed interest payments and convertible medium-term certificates (*Certificati del Tesoro con Opzione – CTO*) to the market for the first time. By 1986, it is also notable that medium-term Treasury bonds had grown substantially from their 1982 proportions, whereas short-term bonds, although rising in absolute terms, no longer represented the proportions of total outstanding debt that they had done in 1982. By the end of 1986 the proportion of outstanding short-term debt (*BOT*) had fallen dramatically to 30 per cent of all debt. In fact the residual life of Italy's debt evolved from an average of 1.13 years in 1982 to 3.88 years in 1986. Thus, since the early 1980s the government has attempted, where the economic conditions permitted, to extend the average life of Italy's debt.

The period 1986 to 1990 saw the average life actually plummet from 3.88 years to 2.5 years. However, this trend was on the whole due to the economic conditions, which effectively dictated such action. The Italian economy was performing very well and thus there were more attractive investment opportunities elsewhere. Moreover, as a result of economic overheating, inflation was fairly high and investors were unwilling to tie their money up for long periods of time. With greater uncertainty in the Italian economy, the differentials on gross yield compared to other countries increased substantially, meaning that it was more expensive for the government to issue long-term debt. However, though the amount of outstanding short-term debt (*BOT*) almost doubled from 183 bn lire in 1986 to 329 bn lire in 1990, the amount of outstanding long-term debt (*BTP*) also rose substantially from 71 bn lire in 1986 to 206 bn lire in 1990, showing the government's commitment to lengthening the life of the public debt.

As of 1991, the government was once again able to fulfil its aim of issuing more medium-term and particularly long-term debt. Although the currency crisis somewhat hindered the completion of this objective, by the end of 1993 *BTPs* (long-term debt) represented 29 per cent of the debt, whereas in 1986 they represented a mere 12 per cent of the total. From 1992 to 1993 this trend continued, the medium- and long-term securities held by the market rose from 46.1 per cent to 49.8

per cent and the proportion of short-term bonds fell from 23 per cent to 20.9 per cent (the remaining part made up of either overseas investment or securities held by the central bank). This evolution meant that at the end of 1993 the average life of outstanding debt was 3.29 years.

With this switch from short- to long-term financing of the public debt came the necessity for a wide variety of bonds, thereby giving further encouragement and greater variety to investors. In fact, December 1993 saw the issue of the first thirty-year bond in Italy, giving Italy a position among the elite in terms of the wide variety of bond products on offer.

4.17 INTERNATIONALIZATION AND INSTITUTIONAL INVESTMENT

The structural reforms that have characterized the Italian bond market during the 1980s and 1990s have paved the way for institutional and overseas investment. By diversifying the currencies in which Italian bonds are denominated, the government has effectively been able to reduce the cost of debt servicing. By 1994, the Italian government has issued bonds denominated in yen, dollars and deutschmarks, all countries with significantly lower interest rates than Italy. However these international bond issues still represented only 3.6 per cent of all outstanding bonds in 1993 (1.6 per cent in 1990). Additionally, the government has been keen to offer bonds denominated in Ecu. As the Ecu is a basket currency the risks for foreign investors involved with fluctuations in the lira exchange rate are minimized. As a proportion of outstanding bonds, the Ecu bond has remained relatively stagnant at around 4–4.5 per cent during the period 1990–3. As a result of these changes Italian bonds denominated in foreign currencies (including Ecu) have risen from 6.0 per cent in 1990 to 7.8 per cent in 1994. It should be noted that during much of 1992 and early 1993, because of the currency crisis, the Italian government had to suspend much of its foreign programme, only for it to pick up in the latter half of 1993 and in early 1994.

The growing attractiveness of Italian Treasury bonds can be shown by the oversubscription of issues in recent years. Short-term bonds (*BOT*) have been oversubscribed by 34 per cent in 1993 as opposed to 25 per cent in 1992. Medium-term Treasury bonds (*CCT*) have been oversubscribed by 106 per cent in 1993 as opposed to 83 per cent in 1992. Long-term Treasury bonds (*BTP*) have been oversubscribed by 81 per cent in 1993 as opposed to 65 per cent in 1992. This increase in demand has been in large part because of greater interest from abroad. The share of debt held by non-residents has risen dramatically in the period 1992–3. In fact *Banca d'Italia* estimates put the figure as high as 10.5 per cent in 1993 compared to 6.3 per cent in 1992. Net purchases from residents have indeed declined from 134 trillion lire in 1992 to 90.3 trillion in 1993, whereas foreign investors made net purchases of government securities totalling 99.6 trillion lire in 1993 compared to 9.7 trillion in 1992.

In the past, Italian government securities have distinguished themselves from those of other industrialized countries in that the majority of bonds have been held by the final investor (individuals, families, businesses) and not by institutions. However, this characteristic is set to change; having reached a peak of 67 per cent in 1990, the proportion of outstanding debt held in 1993 by final investors has fallen to 54 per cent.

4.18 CONCLUDING REMARKS

As long as uncertainty remains concerning the Italian government, the yields of Italian government bond issues will have to remain substantially higher than that of other European countries to attract investment. In this way the premium that the government has to pay for its borrowing requirement can be reduced. During 1993 the differential between gross yields on Italian and German ten-year bonds narrowed from 640 to 310 base points. This differential declined further with the election of Berlusconi in March, and the restoration of business confidence, to stand at 260 points at the end of April. After the honeymoon period was over for the new government, this differential began to rise again with continued uncertainty as to the severity of the 1995 budget and credibility of the government. As a result of the government's stalling on the contents of the budget, the differential rose to 470 basis points by mid-September 1994. Therefore, fiscal austerity holds a double reward; a reduction in the public sector borrowing requirement and a reduction in debt servicing costs due to the subsequent improvement in confidence on the part of the financial markets.

APPENDIX 4A

'A competitive and marginal auction for Italian government bonds', translated from *Guida al Mercato dei Titoli di Stato* from the Italian Treasury, July 1994.

A competitive auction (for *BOT*)

For competitive auctions there is no basic price, therefore all bids above the calculated threshold are accepted, taking account of the size of the issue. The price that was offered by the investor must then be paid.

Imagine a scenario where there is an auction of 1,000 billion *BOTs* and three banks (banks X, Y and Z) taking bids. All prices are in lire.

BANK X	100 bn at 92.5 (yield 8.11 per cent)
	100 bn at 92.0 (yield 8.70 per cent)
	50 bn at 91.95 (yield 8.75 per cent)
	50 bn at 91.0 (yield 9.11 per cent)
	100 bn at 90.0 (yield 11.11 per cent)
BANK Y	50 bn at 92.0 (yield 8.70 per cent)
	50 bn at 91.9 (yield 8.81 per cent)
	50 bn at 91.8 (yield 9.29 per cent)
	50 bn at 91.25 (yield 9.59 per cent)
	100 bn at 91.0 (yield 9.89 per cent)
BANK Z	150 bn at 92.4 (yield 8.23 per cent)
	200 bn at 92.2 (yield 8.46 per cent)
	200 bn at 92.0 (yield 8.70 per cent)
	100 bn at 91.8 (yield 8.81 per cent)
	50 bn at 91.5 (yield 9.29 per cent)

The bids from all the banks are then placed in decreasing order of price until the issue is satisfied:

Price (lire)	Quantity (bn)
92.5	100
92.4	150
92.2	200
92.0	50

Quantity of 500 bn, equivalent to half of the issue
Average weighted price – 92.3

Price (lire)	Quantity (bn)
92.0	300
91.95	50
91.9	50
91.8	150

The bids which satisfy the issue amount to 1,050 bn. This is 50 bn more than the total issue.

The yield for the average weighted price (92.3) of half of the issue is then calculated, which in this case is 8.34 per cent. To this figure 150 basis points are added to give a yield of 9.84 per cent, which corresponds to a price of 91.04. This price then forms the threshold price so that any bids under this level are immediately rejected.

Therefore, in this example, only bids of 91.8 and above are accepted and investors have to pay the price that they bid. However, a problem lies in how to distribute the *BOTs* priced at 91.8, as the demand at that price is 150 bn and there is only 100 bn left to distribute. In such cases, the demand is satisfied proportionally. In this example, this would mean that bank Y, which asked for 50 bn, would receive 33.333 bn, and bank Z, which requested 100,000, would be allocated 66.667 bn.

A marginal auction (for *CCT* or *BTP*)

For marginal auctions, bids are satisfied at the same price once the threshold price has been calculated.

Imagine a situation where 1,000 bn *BTPs* are being issued, again with the participation of three banks (X, Y and Z). Prices are in lire.

BANK X	100 bn at 102.0
	200 bn at 101.8
	200 bn at 99.5
BANK Y	50 bn at 101.8
	100 bn at 101.5
	150 bn at 101
BANK Z	200 bn at 101.5
	300 bn at 101.35
	300 bn at 101.0

The bids from the banks are then placed in decreasing order of price:

Price (lire)	Quantity (bn)
102.0	100
101.8	250
101.5	150
	———
	500

Average weighted price of half of the offer – 101.75

Price (lire)	Quantity (bn)
101.5	150
101.35	300
101.0	450
99.5	200

By subtracting 200 basis points from the average weighted price of half of the offer, a threshold price of 99.75 is obtained. Consequently, only the applications at a price of 99.5 lire are refused. The marginal price is therefore the lowest acceptable price, which in this case is 101 lire. This is the price that everybody pays for the *BTP*. A total of 50 bn bonds will be distributed at a price of 101 lire and this is the reason why this is the marginal price. Since the demand for bonds at a price of 101 lire was actually 450 bn, banks Y and Z have to share the remaining 50 bn bonds. Therefore, bank Y will receive 16.667 bn and bank Z will obtain 33.333 bn.

5 Privatizations

5.1 THE ROAD TO PRIVATIZATION

Italy is, in many respects, a late-comer to the process of privatization. European privatization activities began in the early 1980s in the United Kingdom, and spread throughout western Europe, and then subsequently to central and eastern Europe. Italy presents an almost unique set of favourable conditions for a wide-ranging privatization programme. These are:

- the presence of a large number of state-controlled enterprises, accounting for a substantial proportion of the total value generated by the economy;
- attractive flotation prices given the urgency to raise revenue for the government to curb the expansion of the public debt rapidly;
- ample margins for improving the efficiency and profitability of the newly privatized companies.

The government announced its plans to sell-off many of the state-held companies on 29 January 1992 (Law N. 35). Based on the medium-term plan presented by the government in 1992, the revenue from privatizations was estimated to be about 7,000 billion lire for 1993 (the actual revenue was 3,956 billion lire) and 10 trillion lire for each of the subsequent two years. It has to be stressed that the total receipts from the privatizations could substantially exceed the net revenue allocated to the Treasury, since part of the receipts will be used to reduce the indebtedness of companies owned by *Iri* or *Eni*.

The privatization programme in Italy has explicitly permitted the government to sell majority stakes in state companies. It specifies that budgetary transfer payments to the former publicly owned companies (some of which have now become limited companies) are to be substantially reduced and slowly eliminated. This would gradually enable them to achieve complete financial independence. New rules for public tender have also been established, such as introducing fiscal incentives and the possibility of debt–equity conversion of government securities for the shares of companies that are to be privatized. The declared aim of the government is to achieve the broadest possible ownership base.

The principle of 'financial openness' was established in Italy with the liberalization of capital movements in the late 1980s. This principle has been rigorously adhered to, demonstrating that the Italian authorities are strongly committed to keeping the economy open to cross-border financial transactions. The same principle also applies to the purchase of shares of Italian public sector firms by foreign investors, even if this involves the transfer of ownership abroad. A major role has already been assigned to international financial institutions in various stages of the privatization process, such as the valuation of companies and the placement of their shares.

The programme for the actual sale of publicly owned enterprises in Italy began in 1993. Nevertheless, these privatizations have helped sustain the markets' confidence in the government's efforts to redress the problem of mounting public debt. The privatizations have also fostered greater efficiency both in the stock exchange and within the newly privatized companies themselves. During 1993 important reorganizational measures were introduced within the public sector enterprises that were to be privatized. The aim was to improve their operating efficiency and their financial position as a prelude to privatization. In terms of the number of operations completed and resources involved, the privatization measures adopted in 1993 and in the first few months of 1994 have far exceeded the results achieved during the preceding years. Moreover, public finances benefited directly and indirectly from the privatization programme in terms of the restored confidence created within the domestic and international markets. With respect to allocative efficiency, privatization also encouraged public sector companies to implement restructuring programmes. This led to a sharp fall in staffing levels within these firms, resulting in an improvement in their financial health and productivity.

5.1.1 Market reforms before privatization

The conditions required for carrying out such an ambitious privatization plan have necessitated the adoption of several laws that establish the legal framework within which the process should be carried out.

One of the first measures was the transformation of the four main state holding companies (*Enel* (electricity), *Eni* (petrochemical), *Ina* (insurance) and *Iri* (a holding company controlling public industries and banking conglomerates)) from state-controlled agencies into public limited companies. This was done in order to allow them to obtain a listing on the stock exchange and sell shares to domestic and foreign investors. It also made them subject to the provisions of civil law. The implementation of the programme is now supervised by a Permanent Committee for Privatization, which was set up by the Directive of the Prime Minister of 30 June 1993, which enjoys extensive powers to control and audit all transactions.

In the defence industry and in the area of public utilities (oil and gas, electricity, public transport and telecommunications) the government will retain a stake in the respective companies for a period not exceeding five years in order to protect the company during a period in which the ownership structure, and thus the company itself, is still relatively vulnerable. This decree law was introduced on 27 September 1993, Number 389, for the following reasons:

• to sterilize the voting rights of 'unwelcome' shareholders along the lines of British Petroleum Company (BP) at the time of sale of the UK government's stake in the company;
• to stop shareholders from liquidating the company or deviating from its main line of business, and from moving the headquarters abroad.

In December 1993 (Law 20/12/93 N. 531), the government obtained the right to establish a new regulatory authority (that has not yet been set up) for public utilities. This body was to open the way for the regulation and monitoring of public utilities prices, service quality and the terms governing access to the national network.

This decree was also amended on 31 March 1994 (Number 216). It introduced a set of rules designed to limit individual stakes in companies, to protect minority shareholders and to run shareholders' meetings in organizations with large numbers of shareholders. The decree thus provides scope for giving some of the state-owned financial services companies and public utilities many of the features of 'public companies' – a model non-existent in the Italian industrial landscape up until then.

Such changes were a necessary condition for the privatization of large companies that operate utilities networks. Helped by declining interest rates and measures such as the suspension of capital gains tax, the stock market exploited the opportunity offered by privatization to encourage wider share ownership. It will be possible to consolidate and build upon these results once there is a sufficient number of financial institutions capable of permanently monitoring company ownership.

5.2 PRIVATIZATIONS DURING 1993

The main privatizations during 1993 were as follows (see Table 5.1):

- In March *Eni* sold two companies of the Savio group: *Cognatex* for 22 billion lire and *Matec* for 48 billion lire.
- At the beginning of the year *Efim* engineering group was placed in liquidation. In June the liquidator of *Efim* sold *Siv*, a glass company, to a British group for about 210 billion lire. In the same month, the liquidator transferred *Oto-Melara*, *Officine Galileo*, *Augusta* and other defence industry firms to *Iri's Finmeccanica* group. It also began to restructure the group's railways engineering interests, which include *Breda Costruzioni Ferroviarie*. Finally, *Efim* group has been formally dissolved by Law 33 of 17 September 1993.
- After the failure of a previous bidding round, *Iri* relinquished its 62 per cent stake in *Cirio-Bertolli-DeRica* (310 billion lire) on 7 October 1993.
- In November 1993, *Sme*, *Iri*'s food products and retailing subsidiary company, completed the sale of its 62 per cent controlling stake in *Italgel* to Nestlé for 437 billion lire (the operation started on 6 August 1993).
- On 8 December 1993, *Iri*, the state holding company, sold its 67 per cent stake in *Credito Italiano* (the country's seventh largest bank). It was privatized after a price discount of 9.6 per cent on the last Friday before the flotation. There was also a bonus share (1 for 10) given to all those who took up that week's offer and retained their shares for three years (with a ceiling of 1,500 new shares). The flotation was extremely well received (oversubscription was estimated to be between five and six times). In fact the flotation raised 1,829 billion lire for *Iri* who also offered 17 per cent of the 'savings shares' that could be converted into ordinary shares paying 160 lire each.

5.3 PRIVATIZATIONS DURING 1994

In January *Finmeccanica* (an *Iri* group subsidiary) sold its 100 per cent stake in *Esaote* obtaining 60 billion lire (as is mentioned in Table 5.2

Table 5.1 1993 privatizations

Date	Company	Previous owner	Total amount sold lire (billion)
3/93	Cognetex	Eni	22
3/93	Matec	Eni	48
6/93	Siv	Efim	210
10/93	C/B/DR	Iri	310
11/93	Italgel	Iri	437
12/93	Credit	Iri	1,829

Table 5.2 1994 privatizations

Date	Company	Previous owner	Total amount sold lire (billion)
1/94	Esaote	Iri	60
2/94	Imi	Treas. other	2,200
3/94	Comit	Iri	2,891
4/94	Comm. Term.	Eni	30
5/94	N. Pignone	Eni	1,100
6/94	Ina	Treasury	4,530
7/94	Acciai Sp. Ter.	Iri	600
11/94	GS/Autogrill	Iri	704

along with the other privatizations of 1994). As regards the Treasury's direct shareholding of 33 per cent of *Imi* (medium- and long-term lending, personal financial services and investment banking), it was sold through an oversubscribed public offering for about 2.2 trillion lire in February 1994, reducing the Treasury's interest to about 22.9 per cent. Now three Italian banks *Cariplo, San Paolo di Torino* and *Monte dei Paschi di Siena* are *Imi*'s largest shareholders excluding the Treasury. The Treasury will sell its remaining stake in the coming months of 1994 and *Imi* is studying the possibilities, which could include a direct offer to foreign investors or to reinforce the stake of the 'hard core' Italian banks mentioned above.

Further privatizations were as follows:

- On 1 March 1994 *Banca Commerciale Italiana* was sold by way of a public offering for a total of 2,891 billion lire In each case *Iri* retained just over 3 per cent of the equity, which will be allocated to subscribers who hold their shares for at least three years.

- In April *Eni* sold the last company of the *Savio* group, *Commercializzazione Termodomestici* for 30 billion lire after the other two companies had been sold in March 1993.
- The sale of *Eni*'s (state oil company) controlling interest in *Nuovo Pignone* (gas turbines subsidiary) for 1.1 trillion lire to a consortium of Italian and foreign companies was set in motion in May 1994.
- *Ina* shares began to be traded in Milan, London and New York on 6 July 1994. The 418,000 Italian private investors who applied for shares in the Treasury-owned insurance company received some or all of the shares they asked for, making it the first Italian privatization not to leave at least some shareholders empty-handed. This sale has been the largest Italian privatization to date, and one of the biggest in Europe in the past three years. Advisers pointed out that it was the second most popular Italian sell-off in terms of the number of public applications, and was much bigger than previous sales of stakes in financial institutions: *Credito Italiano*, *Banca Commerciale Italiana* and *Imi*.
- *Acciai Speciali Terni*, one of the companies of the former public steel group headed by *Iri*, was sold on 14 July 1994 for 600 billion lire.
- The two groups of companies owned by *Sme*, *GS* (supermarkets) and *Autogrill* (catering), were launched on the stock market for 704 billion lire by *Iri* on 4 November 1994, after earlier bids were judged to be unacceptable.

5.4 PRIVATIZATIONS FROM 1995

Privatization programmes of the magnitude and complexity of those being carried out in Italy require a reasonable span of time for their completion, in the order of years rather than months. For this reason by the time this study was completed (in the fourth quarter of 1994) only an approximate schedule could be given for the following companies (see Table 5.3).

Table 5.3 Scheduled privatizations, from 1995

Forecast privatizations	Company	Owner	1993 book value lire (billion)
1995–6	Bnl	Treasury	6,575
1995	Ilva Laminati Piani	Iri	1,496

In 1994 preliminary work has been carried out for the privatization of *Bnl, Banca Nazionale del Lavoro* (1993 book value 6,575 billion lire), one of the financial institutions controlled by the Treasury (scheduled privatization for 1995–6). In November 1993 it was decided that *Ilva Laminati Piani* (with a 1993 book value of 1,496 billion lire) will be sold by public auction in 1995. This was a company of the former public steel group headed by *Iri* and now split into three new companies.

On top of these developments, the main privatizations in 1995 will be as follows (see Table 5.4).

Table 5.4 Main privatizations

Date	Company	Owner	%	Book value lire (billion)
Beg. 1995	*Stet*	*Iri*	61	24,000
Spring 1995	*Enel*	Treasury	100	25–35,000
End 1995	*Eni/Agip*	Treasury	100	30–40,000
1995–6	*Cariplo*	Foundation	100	8–10,000

Eni/Agip

While no decision on the privatization strategy for *Eni/Agip* was announced by the time this study was completed (in the fourth quarter of 1994), there could be three possible options:

- The merging of the energy part and engineering segment of the conglomerate into one company (called *SuperAgip*) which could then be floated.
- Floating only *Eni*'s shares with simultaneous asset sales and re-organization of non-core companies.
- Splitting the conglomerate into three companies: energy, chemical and other activities, to be floated individually.

Either *SuperAgip* or the first *Eni* flotation tranche is likely to take place during the last months of 1995. The value of *SuperAgip* is in the range 30,000–40,000 bn lire (at an average P/E ratio of 14.3 for the sector and P/Book ratio of 2.0). In 1993, the consolidated equity of *Eni* was estimated at 16,200 bn lire.

Enel

This company has been entirely owned by the Treasury since its nationalization in 1962. The primary objective of *Enel* is to ensure sufficient power to provide for the development of the country, at the lowest management cost and at the lowest price. As a consequence, it has traditionally had low profits (even though they have doubled in the last six years). However, forecasts for revenues and profitability after the privatization are attractive. This is largely due to the fact that its power utility meets 88 per cent of Italian power demand and *Enel* has 100 per cent country coverage with 12 per cent of power sources coming from abroad. Moreover, the company's production capacity is 51,000 MW, which makes it the third largest electricity utility company in the OECD countries.

Before the privatization (forecast for spring 1995) the following measures have to be introduced.

- a regulatory authority by the government,
- a new tariff plan (price cap) for the company or regulatory authority,
- a rationale for sharing the units and re-allocating capital/personnel,
- a re-examination of the 'Concession Act' (99 years).

Then *Enel* will be either split into three units (production, transport, distribution) and put up for flotation with the production and distribution sectors as a second flotation. The alternative is float the entire company in one lot and then to split it into three units.

Stet

Stet is the controller of *Telecom Italia*, the single provider of telecommunications that has been created for Italy in the privatization programme. The telecommunications sector in Italy is engaged in a massive modernization and expansion programme. Recently this programme was scaled down because of the recession in the early 1990s. In *Stet*'s latest three-year plan (1994–6), the rate of net additions of subscribers to the basic fixed-link network will diminish by around a third from 750,000 per annum to 500,000 per annum.

To escape from the government's financial constraints, and also to conform with the EEC directives, the sector is being prepared to face the rigours of competition, with regulated tariffs for the basic services matched more systematically to costs. Above all, *Stet* is being groomed for privatization – an important source of finance for the government as it struggles to pay off its excessive borrowings. It is also a rare chance for internal telecom giants with an appetite for attractive (though doubtless restricted) strategic stakes in *Telecom Italia*.

Existing and potential investors are clearly keen to know the sector's 'correct' value, and especially to know how far market values for the quoted components diverge from what they should be. Attempts to obtain accurate valuations encounter difficult obstacles, not least the tangled complexity of the sector in its current 'non-rationalized' state. Moreover, certain key items of information (for example the profitability of *Sip*'s cellular operation, and accounting details for the long-distance operator *Iritel*) remain unknown.

The timetable for the restructuring of the sector has been confirmed. The Treasury Ministry and *Stet* itself have stated that its privatization will commence before the beginning of 1995.

Cariplo

Since its foundation, in 1823 in Milan, *Cariplo* has been wholly owned by the *Cariplo Foundation*. Its core market is Lombardy, where it is a dominant player. It is Lombardy's leading savings bank with a well-diversified loan portfolio, but it also contains significant operations outside this core market. Most importantly it is the leader in private client fund management. It has also succeeded in expanding its national network, making it less dependent on this regional base market, by following a three-pronged strategy:

- the absorption of *IBI*,
- increasing the size of its branch network,
- and forming relationships with other savings banks over which *Cariplo* exercises considerable control.

These 'partner' banks represent a huge distribution network which is greatly to *Cariplo*'s advantage. The bank has a strong collection of products to sell through this network, including mutual funds, mortgages and life assurance. These areas could be sources of considerable growth in the near future, because, first, the Italian assurance market is underdeveloped. Second, current levels of state provision for pensions are unsustainable and, last, it has been proven that bank branches are an effective method of selling policies.

5.5 CONCLUSIONS

The success of the privatization plan will depend to a considerable extent on the ability of the stock market to handle the process. The Italian stock exchange, largely located in Milan, will have a crucial role to play. Unlike the market for government securities, which has now reached an advanced stage of development and is highly efficient, the market for private securities in Italy is still relatively thin and in many respects inadequate to meet the needs of a modern industrial country. International comparisons show that Italy is still far behind most other industrial countries in terms of indicators such as the capitalization-to-GDP ratio, the number of domestic companies listed, and so on.

The small size of the stock market conceals the fact that, at the aggregate level, the proportion of equity capital in total financing is high in the Italian business sector. The gross equity issues of unlisted companies rose steadily between 1988 and 1992, totalling about $52 billion in the period. This represents twice the amount raised by listed companies. Moreover, the risk capital represented 44 per cent of company financing in 1992. The peculiarity of the Italian case is that there is a relatively small proportion of limited companies, and even these have a low propensity to seek a listing on the stock exchange.

Thus Italy possesses all the requisites for rapid growth of private savings, entrepreneurial talents and legislation that allows banks to play a leading role in the securities business. Moreover, in the last couple of years Italian financial markets have proved capable of taking steps towards rapid modernization such as the development of a fully telematic spot market for government securities and the success of the new futures market. Additionally, the open-outcry auction system has been gradually replaced by a screen-based continuous auction market, which will be extended to all stocks by next March. This last development has enabled the Milan stock exchange to recapture a sizeable share of business from London's SEAQ and to establish a record for daily turnover on 18 August 1994.

From a financial point of view, the problem of implementing the privatization programme seems to be more a question of the proper organization of financial intermediaries than of the formation of savings. The total volume of outstanding public debt is about nine times the market value of the stock exchange, an unusually large multiple for an industrialized country. It would be sufficient to transform a small fraction of this outstanding debt into shares of what are now public sector companies in order to realize a very ambitious privatization programme.

6   Concluding remarks

Italy has had remarkable achievements in the 1990s despite its mountain of public debt. The structural improvements (as outlined in the Executive Summary included at the beginning of this study) have occurred even though the economy has suffered from a deep recession lasting from the last quarter of 1992 to the end of 1993.

The problem of public finance remains – partly due to the short-term nature and composition of the debt. Some of the state debt will be reaching maturity in 1995 and 1996. Hence, there should be a levelling-off of its size in the second half of the 1990s and a restraining of the steep growth it has experienced in recent years. Italy has always had a quick turnover of governments and hence, with or without Berlusconi, the economic progress of the economy should continue.

The positive trend resulting from the progress Italy has made in many areas should continue – making the future for Italy quite encouraging. Many of the measures taken in the first half of the 1990s will be working their way through the economy in the second half.

References

Banca D'Italia Annual Reports, for the years 1990, 1991, 1992, 1993.

Banca D'Italia Economic Bulletin (1993) (17) October.

Banca D'Italia Economic Bulletin (1994) (18) February.

Bini Smaghi, L., Padoa-Schioppa, T. and Papadia, F. (1994) *The Transition to EMU in the Maastricht Treaty*, Banca d'Italia, May.

Commission of the European Communities (1993a) *The European Economy – Report & Studies, no. 1.*

Commission of the European Communities (1993b) *Growth, Competitiveness, Employment – The Challenges and Ways Forward into the 21st Century.*

Commission of the European Communities (1994a) *Official Journal of the European Communities – Community Initiative concerning the Adaptation of Small and Medium Sized Enterprises to the Single Market Initiative*, no. 94/C 180/03, vol. 37, 1 July.

Commission of the European Communities (1994b) *Official Journal of the European Communities – Guidelines for the Adaptation of the Workforce to Industrial Change Initiative*, no. 94/C 180/09, vol. 37, 1 July.

Confindustria Centro Studi (in Italian), (1993) *Previsioni dell'Economia Italiana: Il Mercato del Lavoro: Forecasts for the Italian Economy: The Labour Market*, December.

Confindustria Centro Studi (in Italian), (1994a) *La Spesa dell'Industria per la Ricerca Scientifica Nel 1991–1993*: Industry Expenditure on Scientific Research in 1991–1993, March.

Confindustria Centro Studi (in Italian), (1994b) *Evoluzione Dei Settori Industriali Nel 1993*: The Development of Industrial Sectors in 1993, May.

Confindustria Centro Studi (in Italian), (1994c) *Produttività e Redditività del Capitale*: Industry Productivity and Profitability, Report XVI, May.

Confindustria Centro Studi (in Italian), (1994d) *Previsioni dell'Economia Italiana: Una Politica per le Piccole Imprese*: Forecast for the Italian Economy: A Policy for Small Businesses, June.

Confindustria Centro Studi (1994e) *The Italian Economy in 1994–1996*, The CSC Mid-Year Forecasts, June.

Conti, V., Hamavi, R. and Scobie, H. M. (eds) (1994) *Bond Markets, Treasury and Debt Management: The Italian Case*, Chapman and Hall, London.

The Italian Treasury (in Italian), (1994a) *Documento Di Programmazione Economico-Finanziaria Relativo Alla Manovra Di Finanza Pubblica Per Gli Anni 1995–97*: The Finance Law for 1995, July.

The Italian Treasury (in Italian), (1994b) *Guida al Mercato dei Titoli di Stato*, July.

Liemt, G. (1992) 'Economic Globalization: Labour Options and Business Strategies in High Labour Cost Countries', *International Labor Review* vol. 45 (29).

OECD Economic Outlook (1993) no. 53, June.

OECD Economic Surveys – Italy (1991).

OECD Economic Surveys – Italy (1994).

Padoa-Schioppa, T. (1993) 'Unemployment Benefits Effects on Employment and Income Distribution: What we should learn from the system of the Cassa Integrazione Guadagni', *Labour*, Autumn.

Padoa-Schioppa, T. (1994) *Adapting Central Banking to a Changing Environment*, Banca d'Italia, March.

Padoa-Schioppa, T. and Saccomanni, F. (1994) *Managing a Market-Led Global Financial System*, Banca d'Italia, July.

Scobie, H. M. (ed.) (1994) *The European Single Market: Monetary and Fiscal Policy Harmonization*, Chapman and Hall, London.

Scobie, H. M. (1995) 'The European Monetary Union, single currency feasible without ERM', *Economic and Financial Review*, vol. 2, no. 2, Summer.

Sigeco (1994) *Privatisation: A New Era for the Italian Market?*, London, September.

Treu, T. (1992) 'Labour Flexibility in Europe', *International Labour Review*, nos 4–5.

Index